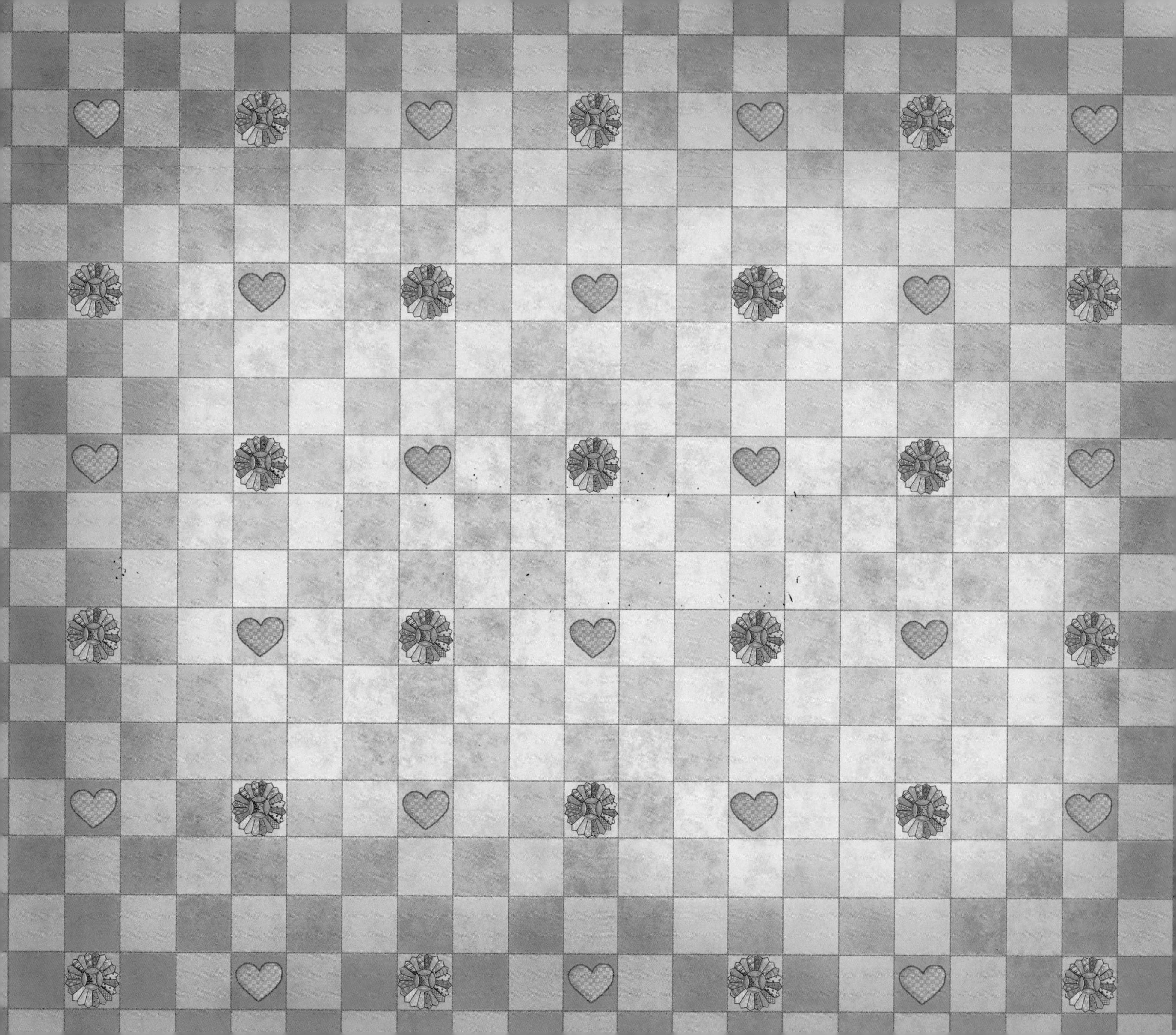

Presented to

My Dear Friend and Sister, Mary

on

Christmas '2002, from Heike

Bless You!!

A Country Sampler of Simple Blessings

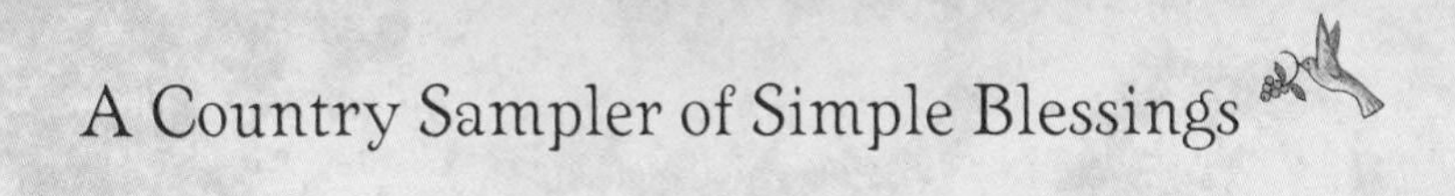

Dedication

For Grandma and Grandpa, Dena and O. T. Bigham,
whose legacy of faith was the cornerstone on which our family was built.
For Mother and Daddy, Juita and Bill Carmack, who let the light of God's love
shine through their lives, giving me an example to follow that was stronger than words.
For my husband, Bob, whose love, prayers, and belief in me make all things possible.
For my children, Christopher Short, Jennifer Short Masi, and Michelle Short—
may you build your own houses on the heritage of faith that
has been handed down through the generations,
and may you pass it on to your children
and your children's children.

But the love of the Lord remains forever with those who fear him.
His salvation extends to the children's children
of those who are faithful to his covenant,
of those who obey his commandments!

Psalm 103:17-18, NLT

And for Ellen Stouffer, whose talent inspires me,
whose words encourage me, and whose friendship warms me.
Without you, there would be no book.

Every time I think of you, I give thanks to my God.

Philippians 1:3, NLT

A Country SAMPLER of Simple Blessings

A collection of homespun stories and paintings celebrating the everyday moments of life

Illustrated by Ellen Stouffer
Written by Peg Carmack Short

Tyndale House Publishers, Inc.
Wheaton, Illinois

Visit Tyndale's exciting Web site at www.tyndale.com

Designed by Jacqueline L. Noe

Typesetting and Production by Ron Kaufmann

Edited by Jan Senn

ISBN 0-8423-5247-3
Printed in China

07 06 05 04 03 02 01
8 7 6 5 4 3

The stories in this collection are based on the author's experiences and memories of life in small Midwestern towns and countrysides, primarily during the 1950s. While most of the stories are based on truth, some of the names and details have been changed when the author deemed it best.

Contents

Acknowledgments

Special thanks to all who contributed the love, support, and spiritual guidance that made this book possible,
including: my grandchildren, Alexis, Adrien, Jared, Isaac, and Silas Short, and Sebastiano Masi,
who bring inspiration and joy to every day;
my sister, Judy French, for all her fact-finding, memory prodding, love, and support;
my good friend Becky Brandvik, director of product development, for giving me this opportunity
and providing her encouragement and considerable talent to make this book become a reality;
my publisher, Doug Knox, for providing leadership and paving the way;
all my friends at Tyndale House, for their encouragement and help;
Jackie Noe and Justin Ahrens, for making the book so beautiful;
my editor, Jan Senn, for her caring, insights, and talent that made this a better book;
all my Carmack and Bigham relatives, who provided the legacy of family, love,
and wonderful memories that make up much of this book;
my "other family"—the Popilchaks, for their lives of faith and the love they give me;
Bill Stouffer, for sharing Ellen and befriending Bob; DeWanna and Joe Oliver, Terry and Jan Stevens,
and all my many other "prayer warrior" friends who kept me and this book in their prayers throughout its writing;
and Helen Carrington, Pauline Brayfield, and the many other friends
and members of Third Baptist Church who have helped me grow spiritually over the years.

Introduction

As far back as I can recall, both my mother and grandmother liked to do what they called "fancy work." With needle, thread, and yarn they worked beautiful magic on quilts, pillowcases, and dresser scarves. They revered this gentle art and tried to hand down their knowledge to me, but I could never quite master the tiny stitches.

Nonetheless, I've always loved the beauty of needlework, and I've particularly admired the delicate stitches and intricate designs found in American country samplers. These works of art, with their pastoral landscapes and pretty gardens, preserved scenes of early American life. Their alphabet borders, printed numerals, moral inscriptions, and favorite Scriptures served as lessons in reading and arithmetic and taught important character values and virtues. Even the definitions of the term *sampler*—an "example to be followed," or "a piece worked by young girls for improvement"—speak to the teaching value of this type of needlework as well as its beauty.

For seventeen years Ellen Stouffer has been re-creating country samplers with paint and brush rather than with needle and thread. Combining promises from Scripture with picturesque scenes of her rural Indiana home and warm memories of family and friends, Ellen weaves a rich tapestry that serves as her own example to be followed and learned "for improvement."

Her paintings invite us to travel down winding country roads to places where folks rest on wide, welcoming porches, greet their neighbors on warm summer evenings, and share the blessing of friendship. They recall memories of quiet nights, interrupted only by the croaking of frogs and the whistle of the 9:47 as it clicks and rattles over the tracks on its way into town. They remind us of silent vistas where millions of stars sparkle like crystals in the nighttime sky and where, as David says in Psalm 19, the heavens speak to us "without a sound or a word," and "tell of the glory of God."

Just as the American country samplers of long ago taught important life lessons to young girls, Ellen's samplers speak to my heart in a special way. They remind me of the small Midwestern town where I grew up and of visits to my father's boyhood home in the Missouri Ozarks. There, in those serene and peaceful surroundings, I learned much of what remains important to me today: my faith in God; my love of family, friends, and home; and my delight in simple pleasures—the beauty

of a rose, the rushing sound of a mountain stream, or the scent of the air after a spring rain.

Today my life seems filled with constant busyness—so much so that it is often difficult for me to take time to be quiet and listen as God speaks to me.

Two verses from one of Ellen's samplers speak to the longing of my heart: "Come to me, all of you who are weary and carry heavy burdens, and I will give you rest" (Matt. 11:28, NLT) and "Thou wilt keep him in perfect peace, whose mind is stayed on thee" (Isa. 26:3, KJV). Those are promises I cling to as I seek to spend more time alone with God.

If you are longing for a little rest and peace, I invite you to travel with me to Ellen Stouffer's countryside, where gardens bloom with snowdrops in March and asters in October. Where aromas of wood smoke, freshly baked cobbler, and fried chicken mingle. And where friends and neighbors gather for good food and easy conversation. Here, among tall trees, beside rocky creeks, and atop grassy knolls, God speaks to us through everyday miracles.

Ellen and I invite you to look with new eyes and see in every sampler and in each homespun tale a simple blessing just waiting to be discovered.

you will go out in joy and be led forth in peace; the mountains and hills will burst into song before you, and all the trees of the field will clap their hands
Isaiah 55:12
Peace And Plenty
ellen Stouffer © 1993

Talks in Tall Trees

You will go out in joy and be led forth in peace; the mountains and hills will burst into song before you, and all the trees of the field will clap their hands.

ISAIAH 55:12, NIV

When autumn breezes began to send leaves sailing through the air and plump pumpkins were starting to burst from the vines, it was time for our family to return to the Missouri Ozarks, where my dad was born. There we marked the passing of summer by viewing the miracle of changing leaves. The view grew more spectacular as we drove west beyond St. Louis. The roads became steeper and the trees more dense as the path wound its way through the mountains.

The road we traveled was Route 66, which snaked past campgrounds, Burma-Shave signs, and billboards advertising tourist attractions such as Jesse James's hideout and Onondaga Cave.

Most of the time we arrived late at night. My sister and I would stumble out of the car, tousle-headed and groggy from sleep. Soon we were embraced by a chorus of exuberant voices as aunts, uncles, and cousins surrounded us. Strong arms circled us and pulled us close. There were sweet kisses, followed by exclamations of "My, look how big you've grown!"

My dad and his brothers exchanged slaps on the back and bear hugs. Laughter bubbled up around us like an explosion from Old Faithful. Secure in the love and legacy of my father's past, I was lulled by the dancing voices and the warm camaraderie of my Missouri relatives. Despite my excitement at being in the country for a few days, I soon fell asleep, cocooned in a feather bed and sung to sleep by crickets and cicadas.

The next morning I awoke early to the sounds of my father rising. Quickly and quietly I threw on my clothes and tiptoed down to the kitchen. I wanted to be the only one up, certain that Daddy would take me for a walk in the woods. I loved being alone with my dad because he was a great storyteller and my hero.

Sharing conspiratorial whispers, we packed a thermos of hot cocoa, which Daddy made especially for me. Then we climbed into our used Plymouth and set out for our early-morning adventure.

The roads grew increasingly rough and rocky as we left the main highway and headed into the surrounding countryside. We were off to see the family farm of my father's youth and to take a walk in the nearby woods. Finally the road narrowed to a mere footpath, and there we parked and began our communion among tall oaks and shag-

bark hickories. The air was perfumed with the smell of apples from a nearby orchard and wood smoke from a neighboring cabin. Around us the morning mist kissed mountains and meadows, and the trees sighed with our passing. Here, amid a kaleidoscope of amber, crimson, and golden leaves, my father told me about growing up on a farm in the Ozarks.

He pointed out a distant hilltop where there was a deserted church and an ancient grave site. In hushed tones he told me a shivers-down-the-spine story handed down from his father. The tall tale chilled and thrilled me the way a good mountain story should. Of course, he assured me, these stories were just fun to tell and weren't really true.

He taught me the names of trees and showed me the fine points of mountain medicine by pointing out flowers and roots his mother had told him made good medicines when brewed as teas. And he warned me never to eat wild berries, onions, or mushrooms unless he was with me as a guide because some were poisonous.

We gathered hickory nuts from the ground and placed them in the deep pockets of my father's jacket. Then we rested at the crest of a hill under a tall, stately tree.

"Do you know that trees have intuition?" my father asked me.

Intrigued by the thought, I shook my head. "No."

"When a tree feels threatened by disease, drought, or fire," he told me, "it begins to twist itself under the bark, reinforcing itself so it becomes stronger.

"We're a lot like that tree," he said. "As we go through life, we face danger and hardship. Disease and the strong winds of trouble threaten to destroy us. But in the same way God designed protection for the trees so they would survive hard times, he uses our struggles to help us become stronger. But always remember," he cautioned, "that in the midst of our trials, God never leaves us. If we keep our eyes on him and trust his guidance, then, just like these trees, we'll grow stronger."

From that day on, I've never seen a stately oak without wondering how much it might have struggled and persevered in order to become grand and majestic. And while I would like my life always to be joyous and free of trouble, I remember my father's words and the Scripture verse he taught me: "Whenever trouble comes your way, let it be an opportunity for joy. For when your faith is tested, your endurance has a chance to grow. So let it grow, for when your endurance is fully developed, you will be strong in character and ready for anything" (James 1:2-4, NLT).

Once again the trees have turned to amber and a sudden brisk breeze yanks open my jacket, reminding me that winter is not too far away. As I take a morning walk in the woods near my home, the dewy grasses dampen my feet and brambles tug at my pant leg. I hear the noisy cawing of scolding crows, angry that I've disturbed their morning meal. The wind blows and the leaves of the trees rustle and seem to clap their hands. And my heart is filled with joy as I remember my father and our walks in the woods.

I've long since forgotten the names of the trees and which plants make the best medicine. Yet my father's love for God and his daily example of faithfulness, through good times and bad, walk with me always.

He keeps His eyes upon you as you come and go. Psalms 121:8

Passages of the Heart

He keeps his eye upon you as you come and go.

PSALM 121:8, TLB

It was 1955—long after the golden age of train travel. But in the sleepy little town of Crocker, Missouri, where many of my cousins lived, the rail lines still flourished. Frequently we were forced to wait at the railroad crossing as the speeding trains flew by, their freight cars filled with barley and corn, steel and aluminum, and a multitude of other cargoes heading to and from large industrial areas like St. Louis, Chicago, and Detroit. My sister and I would make a game of counting the cars. Sometimes they numbered well over one hundred.

But the trains that excited me most were the sleek silver passenger trains that rumbled and rattled their way into town from places unknown. I used to sit on the front porch of my uncle's house and fantasize about where they were going or where they might have been. Late at night I'd lie in bed and listen to the whistle's lonesome wail, and I'd dream about where the trains might take me someday.

But it wasn't until my junior year in high school that I had my first chance to ride the rails.

Our school's choral group, of which I was a member, was invited to perform on a radio program called the "Chicago Breakfast Club." This event was combined with a class trip to the Windy City, and we traveled by train from St. Louis to Chicago.

By then train travel had fallen on hard times. And while I expected a dining car boasting the opulence of the Orient Express, what I found was more like the lunch counter at Woolworth's. But my momentary disappointment didn't keep me from longing for adventure. I remained eager to see what the world held in store beyond the confines of my hometown.

Perhaps my desire to explore the world outside my window was inherited from my father. For most of his boyhood, he never traveled beyond the boundaries of the small towns that surrounded his Ozark mountain home. So he eagerly grasped the opportunity when he was

offered what sounded like an exciting job. He was nineteen and working as a night desk clerk in a drowsy little Missouri hotel. While there, he was approached by a detective agency and offered a position as an investigator. His first assignment was to find and follow a former hotel guest—a traveling salesman my father remembered well. The man's wife, who suspected her husband had been straying, had hired the detective firm to follow him.

The assignment required that my dad travel by train to St. Louis for surveillance. Years later, he'd joke about that trip. He'd say that after spending a day in Union Station—browsing all the shops and looking at the crowds of people scurrying back and forth—he was sure he'd seen all of St. Louis, so the next day he just turned around and went home!

That punch line always brought a big laugh, but I found the real truth more exciting. Daddy located the man he was to follow, but the man recognized Daddy, too. The salesman quickly figured out he was being spied on, and he angrily confronted my dad by waving a gun around and shouting threats. Right then Daddy decided that maybe being a detective really wasn't his calling. He turned and quickly headed for the hills of home. As he was fond of saying, his days as a detective were rather short-lived!

Still, the longing to wander runs strong in our family. My own children are travelers and adventurers; they've visited many places in the United States and ventured to romantic foreign destinations such as Paris, Venice, and Rome. And they've had their own share of excitement.

Recently, while on a trip to San Remo, in the Italian Riviera, my two daughters went sightseeing one afternoon. They drove up into the mountains to find a beautiful cathedral they'd heard about. On the way, the road became steeper, narrower, and more winding. Halfway up the mountain, they suddenly came upon a sign that said "Danger—Road Closed." However, just a short distance ahead they could see the town they wanted to visit nestled into the hillside. Since there wasn't a good place to turn around and they couldn't detect any reason for the sign, they decided to ignore it and continue up the mountain.

Suddenly they rounded a hairpin curve—and there was no more road! It just dropped off into space, completely destroyed by a landslide. They were terrified that the rest of the road would crumble beneath them and were afraid to get out of the car. Unfortunately, one of them finally had to get out to direct the other as she drove back down the road and out of danger.

Now they can joke about it, but both say, "If you're ever in Italy and see a sign that says, 'Road Closed,' believe it!"

Hearing this story, I was tempted to ask,

"Why didn't you follow the warning signs in the first place?" But I think I understand.

At times in my own life I'm so intent on my destination that I completely ignore the warning signs along the way that say: "Stop," "Turn Back," "Danger Ahead!" Too often, only when some catastrophe befalls do I pray for God to protect and guide me.

But I'm grateful God is always watching over me. One of my favorite passages of Scripture reminds me: "O Lord, you have examined my heart and know everything about me. You know when I sit down or stand up. You know my every thought when far away. You chart the path ahead of me and tell me where to stop and rest. Every moment you know where I am. . . . Point out anything in me that offends you, and lead me along the path of everlasting life" (Ps. 139:1-3, 24, NLT).

It's been a long time since that little girl sat on the front porch of a peaceful Missouri town, watching the trains and dreaming of unknown places. The heyday of railway travel is long over, and the wealthy elite have given up luxurious private cars in favor of leather seats on the Concorde. Even ordinary folks seem to favor the roar and speed of a jumbo jet over the hiss and romance of the locomotive.

I often wonder what our hurry is. Like my dad and my daughters, I've come to realize that often it isn't reaching our destination that's most important, but what we learn along the way.

ABCDEFGHIJKLMNOPQRSTUVWXYZ
THE FARMHOUSE STUDIO
TAR HEELS
Chapel Hill
I will lift my eyes
unto the hills from
whence cometh
my help.
Little Women
His faithfulness goes on and on to each generation
Psalm 100
Your hand will guide me, your strength will support me.
Ford
A-C

Echoes from the Porch

His faithfulness goes on and on to each succeeding generation.

PSALM 100:5, TLB

When I recall childhood memories of home, my thoughts often turn to our porch, where I spent quiet summer evenings relaxing on the swing with my father. We'd sit in companionable silence, his hand holding mine, while the soft summer evening gathered around us.

My favorite time was dusk, when the heat of the day began to wane and the sharp edges of the landscape blurred into the gathering purple twilight. While the call of crickets harmonized with the creaking of the porch swing, we would sit and talk about anything and nothing. Mostly Daddy listened as I shared my dreams.

My head was full of my own stories, and I told him that when I grew up I was going to be a writer. Although the idea must have amused him (because in the fifties it was ordained that good Midwestern girls become wives and mothers), I don't recall that he ever tried to discourage me. What I do remember is his rapt attention, sweet smile, and gentle indulgence.

Even when Daddy and I didn't talk much, I loved just sitting and listening to the squeak of the chain as the swing went back and forth. Sometimes he would pat my hand or gently run his hand down one of my long braids.

From inside we could hear the clank of dishes being washed and put away and the soft hum of voices as my mother and older sister, Judy, shared their day over washed pots and gleaming china. I loved these quiet times when Judy and I had a few private moments—she with Mother, me with Daddy.

Later Mother would join us on the swing, and Judy would sit on the edge of the porch, dangling her legs over the side. Sometimes Judy would indulge me in a little game of catching fireflies and placing them in a bottle. Then after a while we'd rejoin our parents on the porch, and we'd laugh at a funny story about a practical joke one of Daddy's friends had played on someone at work, or hear news Mother had learned from Grandma or one of her sisters.

One of those stories became part of our family lore, and we all still

laugh about it. It was about the time Grandma got upset by a letter from Aunt Tillie that said, "Stevie got his finger stuck in a tin can this week, and we had to cut it off." Grandma was frantic until she called and found out it was the can they cut off, not Stevie's finger!

Those stories were our entertainment in an era before the TV set replaced conversation. We were one of the last families on the block to have a television because my mother seemed to have a premonition that it would become a shrine, and family life would be sacrificed at its feet. So instead of watching TV, we talked, we listened, and we dreamed. While I don't remember all the conversations exactly, I do remember a sense of peacefulness and of belonging to something wonderful, secure, and solid.

Most houses of the past had big porches, and almost all country homes boasted them. On those porches, families conducted much of the business of life. Babies sunned there on quiet Sunday afternoons while their parents sat nearby, drinking lemonade and talking about whether the price of corn would go up or down that year and whether investing in a new tractor was a good idea. Bored, housebound children were sent there on rainy days to have make-believe tea parties or to build forts from card tables covered with worn-out sheets. And evenings found young lovers courting on porch swings, each of them dreaming about what life had in store.

Today many newly constructed houses have replaced wide, welcoming porches with back decks. Compared to a proper porch—furnished with broad, comfy rockers and slowly swaying porch swings—decks seem as ungainly and uninviting as an opera singer at a hoedown. And front porches have become so small they don't invite friends and neighbors to linger. They seem to shout, "Don't get comfortable! Don't stay too long! I'm busy!"

Lately I've been thinking a lot about focusing on the things in my life that really matter. Perhaps that's why

my thoughts have drifted back to those times on the porch with my father when there was contentment and ease. Because I grew up with a kind, caring earthly father, it's easy for me to grasp the concept of a loving heavenly Father. "The Lord is like a father to his children, tender and compassionate to those who fear him. . . . His salvation extends to the children's children" (Ps. 103:13, 17, NLT). But sometimes I don't spend enough time with him. My life has been stuck in high gear for years as I chase after this thing and that, and often the noise of my whirring around is so loud in my ears that I can't hear God speak to me. No wonder I'm often uncertain about the decisions I make and feel shaky about my choices.

My spiritual life could use a front porch. I need to crawl into my Father's arms and let him wrap himself around me. I need to rest in his love and talk with him about my hopes, my dreams. And I want to wait quietly while he shares the plans he has for me.

Today, when the first rays of light were dawning and the birds were singing wake-up calls, I settled down in a favorite armchair to read Psalm 103. The words reminded me that all I really need, God has provided: forgiveness of sins, healing of disease, and love and tender mercies (vs. 3-4).

I think today I'll throw away my "to do" list. I'm going to spend a little time just resting and waiting on the Lord. Maybe tomorrow I'll talk with my husband about tearing off the deck in favor of a wraparound porch with room for a swing and a rocker or two. And I'll add some red potted geraniums and perhaps a "Welcome" sign to grace the front door. I want to spend more time with family and friends than I have been lately. And God and I need more time to rest in companionable silence and share our love.

ABCDEFGHIJKLMNOPQRSTUVWXYZ
VICTORIA
YARN
BUTTONS
50¢
BUTTONS
NEEDLES
No 5/10
SHARPS
ENGLAND
THREAD
ellen stouffer ©1997
1 2 3 4 5 6 7 8 9 10 11 12 13 14 15 1
God has given each of you some special abilities; use them to help each other.
L.B. 1 Peter 4:10

Stitches in Time

God has given each of you some special abilities; be sure to use them to help each other.

1 PETER 4:10, TLB

W*hir, hum, whir*—most days, those were familiar sounds in our house. They were the sounds of my mother's sewing machine as she stitched curtains and draperies; dresses, skirts, and blouses; napkins, tablecloths, and slipcovers; and an assortment of other things to make our home and us look better. I can still see my mother hunched over the machine, humming a favorite hymn such as "Rock of Ages" as she created rows of straight, precise seams on waists and bodices. Sometimes, long after my sister and I had gone to bed, we could still hear the hum of her sewing machine as Mother eagerly finished her latest project.

Mother had a real gift for fashion and home decor. She studied magazines and visited upscale model homes and then adapted and modified patterns to make her own creations. With my mother's keen eye for style and her talent for sewing, we lived as though we were much more affluent than my father's modest salary allowed.

For my mother, however, sewing wasn't just a way to save money and have more. My mother truly loved to sew, and it showed. No one ever described her creations as "home-made." Instead they were referred to as "handcrafted"—a distinction I learned to appreciate. Each stitch was made with care, and those that weren't precise enough were taken out and replaced until they were perfect. Each piece was neatly ironed before she moved on to the next step. Garments and household items were made with more attention to detail than speed. And in these precise details lay the difference between my mother's sewing and that of other seamstresses I have seen.

It wasn't until I was much older that I understood there were lessons about life stitched into my mother's sewing. When she started to teach my sister and me how to sew, she taught us as much about character as she did about craft.

We learned to place pattern pieces on the fabric carefully in order to conserve as much as possible. "Waste not, want not," she said.

If something didn't lay quite right, I'd be tempted to iron it into place, but she'd always make me tear it out and do it over until it was

right. I can still hear her saying, "If it's worth doing, it's worth doing well."

She never told us a pattern we wanted to make was too advanced. Instead, she taught us not to be afraid to try new and difficult things. "If at first you don't succeed, try, try again," she said.

"Pattern directions were included for a reason," she told us. And she stressed that before she would help us with a problem, we were to take the time and effort to figure things out for ourselves. "Patience is a virtue," she reminded us.

Mother also taught us to mend, and we were never allowed out of the house with a seam or a strap that was pinned. "A stitch in time saves nine," was her favorite rejoinder when I complained about taking off a garment to do a small repair.

Not all the lessons came in the form of adages, however. Once, for a 4-H project, all the girls had to sew the same pattern—a skirt and a square scarf that could be folded and worn as a shawl. I couldn't imagine how they could possibly judge these carbon copies. Other than our choice of fabrics, the outfits all looked the same.

On presentation day, each girl was to model her outfit for the judge. All the girls wore their shawls as shown in the illustration on the pattern cover—folded in half with the point down the middle of their back, the scarf hugging their shoulders and the ends knotted in the middle. I intended to wear mine the same way. But a few minutes before I was to go on, Mother rearranged my shawl. First she draped the point over one shoulder and molded and shaped the fabric to form a graceful cowl. Next she secured the two ends with a brooch and then arranged them over my other shoulder. While the other girls' outfits were identical, mine suddenly had style.

I won first place! I've never deluded myself that this prize repre-

sented my ability as a seamstress. Instead I think my mother should have won, because she had the vision to interpret the garment in her own way. If there were some adage to apply to this lesson, perhaps Mother would have paraphrased Thoreau: "March to the beat of a different drummer. . . . Step to the music you hear."

Over the years I watched my mother's talents as a seamstress grow. She tackled progressively more difficult projects. She learned to create men's suits and coats as skillfully as a tailor. She moved from slipcovers to upholstering and learned to do both like a professional. And when my sister got married, instead of a flower girl's dress, Judy wanted the little girl dressed as a miniature bride. So Mother made a small bridal gown that was an exact duplicate of my sister's—right down to the last seed pearl. Even the bridal shop owner said you could not tell the difference between the child's gown and the original. She said it looked as though the manufacturer had made it.

Now that I'm grown, I see my mother's gift for sewing much like the Bible story about the talents (Matt. 25:14-30). God gave her many gifts: an eye for color and design, a skill for using her hands, a desire for making the most of what she had. Each of these gifts she used, honed, and refined. Over the years these talents grew, and God blessed her.

I know my mother's sewing brought her joy. She made many wonderful creations she was proud of. But besides being an excellent seamstress, she was an excellent mother—one who invested a great deal of time, patience, and love in her parenting. I hope she thought those sewing lessons paid off. And I hope she considered my sister and me her best creations.

GIVE US THIS DAY OUR DAILY BREAD
STOUFFER DAIRY
BUTTER & EGGS
PUMPKINS
The Lord's Prayer Matt. 6:11

Leftovers

Give us this day our daily bread.
MATTHEW 6:11, NKJV

"Come and get it!" That happy call and the ring of the dinner bell frequently summoned me to Aunt Betty's table, where I was sure to be met with a feast.

Aunt Betty wasn't really a relative but an old family friend, and we'd often visit at her farm. Arriving there, I was always greeted by the unfamiliar smell of livestock—a none-too-pleasant scent for a child more familiar with bus fumes than cow manure. But I quickly forgot about the outdoor odor, for inside Aunt Betty's home the aroma was heavenly. It smelled of freshly baked cinnamon rolls and pies hot out of the oven. My mouth started watering as soon as I crossed the threshold, and I couldn't wait until we sat down to eat.

I wasn't the only one who loved Aunt Betty's cooking. She was known far and wide as the best cook in the county. And I'm sure the members of First Street Methodist Church felt especially blessed to have her as a part of their congregation, for Aunt Betty was certain to bring the most popular dish to the Wednesday night potluck supper.

Everyone loved her chicken and dumplings, light-as-air biscuits, egg-batter-fried chicken, and melt-in-your-mouth cobblers and pies. All these delicious foods were created with ingredients from Aunt Betty's farm: rich cream, freshly churned butter, and eggs laid by her hens. In an era when the word *bites* only made people think of forkfuls of food, Aunt Betty was the country equivalent of Julia Child.

It wasn't surprising, then, that every visiting pastor, evangelist, or missionary home on furlough was invited to Aunt Betty's house for Sunday dinner. With the attention due a visiting dignitary, Aunt Betty prepared for their visits with tender care. She would select the ripest, juiciest, and largest fruits and vegetables from her garden. Summertime fare was sure to include fresh tomatoes, corn on the cob, and green beans cooked with new potatoes. The main course included roast beef, smoked ham, and her famous fried chicken. Fresh bread or biscuits waited to be slathered with butter and homemade jams or apple butter. And when her guests finally leaned back in their chairs and patted their bellies, Aunt Betty would say, "Surely you have room for some peach cobbler or fried pies, or maybe you'd like a little bit of both?"

Word quickly spread from West Virginia to Walla Walla and Peoria to Pango Pango that if you made a visit to Pinkneyville, Illinois, there was no better table to put your feet under than Aunt Betty's.

I was sure that if tables could talk, hers would be moaning and groaning. I once asked her why she always worked so hard and spent so much time cooking, and she told me it was her way of showing people how much she cared for them.

Although I'm sure Aunt Betty made everyone feel special, she always made me feel I was her favorite child. At her house she seemed to meet my every need.

Only one time did Aunt Betty show me her disfavor. By then I was grown and engaged to be married. I was anxious for Aunt Betty to meet my soon-to-be husband, and I called her to see if we could drive down for a Sunday afternoon visit. Since I was old enough to understand the hard work that went into making company dinners, I told her we'd be happy with anything—even leftovers.

After a long pause, Aunt Betty informed me that never in her life had she served a guest leftovers, and I was not going to be the first!

"God never chose to bless me with beauty or riches, but he gave me a green thumb, a strong back, and a real knack for findin' my way around a kitchen," Aunt Betty told me. "Even in the worst of times, no one ever visited my home and went away hungry. God always provided hens that laid lots of eggs, a dairy cow for milk and butter, and plenty of produce in the garden. And I thank him for that! I may not be much, but as long as I have a breath left in this ol' body, I'll keep on givin' the best I have."

These days I often find myself thinking about Aunt Betty in amazement. All her life she seemed to work so hard, but I never heard her complain about being too busy or too tired. Before Aunt Betty could bake a cake, she had to milk her cow and churn her own butter, while I live in the quick-and-easy world of toaster waffles, instant mashed potatoes, and fast-food restaurants. Yet I often

grumble about all the work I have to do. And even though I have a bread maker, a dishwasher, and a microwave, I still feel pressed for time.

Sometimes I lose sight of the blessings in my life and fail to thank God for his abundant provision. And some days I serve up my prayer time in five-minute increments while I eat a fast-food burger in my car. But remembering Aunt Betty, I realize that's a lot like giving God the leftovers of my time and my life.

I think it's time I take a few lessons from Aunt Betty and start giving my best to God.

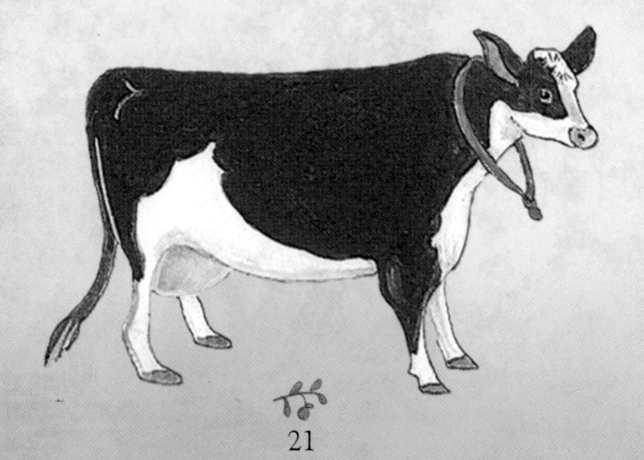

ABCDEFGHIJKLMNOPQRSTUVWXYZ
COME TO PLAY ON ARBOR DAY
LET YOUR ROOTS GROW DOWN
INTO THE SOIL OF GOD'S LOVE
Ephesians 3:17

From Strong Roots

May your roots go down deep into the soil of God's marvelous love.

EPHESIANS 3:17, TLB

The tree-lined street where I grew up was in a quiet residential neighborhood that boasted neat brick and frame houses, some sporting awnings and flower boxes, all with rolling, well-manicured lawns. Next door to our house was a vacant lot, which the neighborhood children had claimed for their summer baseball diamond. Occasionally I could be persuaded to join them in a game, but often I preferred being left alone to think and dream.

My favorite hideaway was up in the branches of the cherry tree that graced our backyard. It was much larger and stronger than most trees of its kind, and my family jokingly referred to it as "the world's largest cherry tree." Unlike most of its smaller cousins, our tree was large enough to extend well over the roof of our garage. Sturdy limbs branched out from both sides—one perfect for the rope swing that my father made for me, the other ideal for hoisting myself up to sit in the branches.

Even though nearby dogs barked, birds and squirrels chattered, lawn sprinklers droned, and an occasional rickety truck rattled down the busy street behind me, I was able to sit up in the cherry tree in relative quiet, safely hidden by its leafy branches. Sometimes I stayed up there for hours, daydreaming or trying to figure out the world around me.

Sometimes I puzzled over the expressions I heard grown-ups use, such as when Mr. Johnson told Daddy the Moran boy had "gotten himself into a pickle." Danny Moran was our neighborhood bully, and he was always doing something mean like running up and pulling my braids so hard he made me cry. So whatever "getting into a pickle" was, I was certain Danny deserved the blame.

The adults I knew often used idioms when they spoke. Someone was always "jumping on the bandwagon," "pouring money down the drain," "making a silk purse out of a sow's ear," or "robbing Peter to pay Paul." What a funny language they seemed to have! But whenever I asked my older sister, Judy, about it, she'd just laugh and say, "Oh, you take everything too literally."

I didn't want to be laughed at, so I quit asking, but I still questioned many

things. I wondered if a small-town girl like me could go to New York to become a writer like the girls in my books, *Peggy Covers the News* and *Jean Craig in New York*. Other times I thought about becoming a missionary like Lottie Moon and living somewhere exotic such as Africa or China. Did ordinary people like me really get to do extraordinary things? If so, maybe I could become a detective and solve mysteries like my favorite girl sleuth, Nancy Drew. Although the closest I ever got to being a detective was the day I found our neighbor's cat hiding in the eaves of our garage, small details like that didn't keep me from thinking, pretending, and dreaming.

Now that I'm grown and able to reflect on my childhood memories, I realize it wasn't the cherry tree that nurtured my dreams. The tree was simply a resting place. The real safe haven of my youth was the unconditional love and constant encouragement my parents gave me. My parents' lives were deeply rooted in the soil of God's love, and they passed that heritage to me. From those strong roots I was able to grow up straight and sturdy.

In many ways, I haven't changed much from that little girl who loved living through the pages of her favorite books. When I grew up, I did go to New York, where I worked at a publishing house for a while. And there's still nothing I find quite so relaxing as escaping through the pages of a novel—however, I've traded heroines from girl sleuth Nancy Drew to private investigator Kinsey Millhone. Although I no longer wonder about silk purses and sow's ears or what I'll be when I grow up, I still spend lots of time asking questions. These days I grapple with why good people have to suffer and why our life on earth is so short. And I still wonder how ordinary people like me can make a difference.

With all of life's complexities, I need a resting place even more than when I was younger—a place to retreat from the busyness of my world and reflect

on more eternal things. The Bible assures me that God's love is such a resting place: "How precious is your unfailing love, O God! All humanity finds shelter in the shadow of your wings" (Ps. 36:7, NLT).

I will always cherish my memories of childhood and those dreams in the branches of the old cherry tree. And I will be forever grateful to my parents for teaching me where to put my trust. God is my real refuge, and I rest in his arms now.

. . .Blessed are the pure in heart, for they shall see God.
Blessed are the peacemakers, for they shall be called sons of God
Matthew 5:8,9
the PIECE MAKER
1995
Seurat Thread
ellen stouffer © 1993

The Piecemakers

Blessed are the peacemakers: for they shall be called the children of God.

MATTHEW 5:9, KJV

My maternal grandparents spent most of their lives moving from house to house. As a child, I didn't consider this odd or even unusual, for that was just how my grandparents lived. Grandpa was a Southern Baptist preacher on Sundays, but the other six days of the week he made his living as a contractor. As part and parcel of this livelihood, he made a habit of buying old, rundown houses and fixing them up. During the renovation, the house would serve as home to my grandparents. Once the work was completed, they would sell the house, move, and start the process all over again.

I'm not sure how Grandma felt about this nomadic lifestyle, but my mother always said both her parents liked it. And they seemed happiest when they had just moved to a new "fixer upper." Perhaps Grandma, like Grandpa, enjoyed the challenge of bringing life back into an old place.

My memories of my grandmother include the fact that she was a strong-minded woman. Not one to sit back and bask in my grandfather's shadow, she knew how to speak her mind—and often did. Her conversation was peppered with strong opinions, frequent adages, and familiar Scriptures—all aimed at keeping her family on the right path. Part of our family lore is her reaction the first time she met my dad, whom she later came to adore. He was twenty-four, and she thought him much too old for her sixteen-year-old daughter. His natural quiet and reserve only added to her suspicion of him. "Still water runs deep and the devil's at the bottom," she warned my mother—who, fortunately for me, chose that time to disregard her mother's advice.

That same spunk and fire helped Grandma raise eight children, labor with Grandpa to start new churches, and help out financially by wallpapering houses during the Depression. She taught Sunday school, helped out friends and neighbors, and quoted long passages of poetry with ease. She loved to sing, and I still sing my grandchildren the songs she sang first to my mother and then to me.

But one of my strongest recollections is that she made beautiful

things out of nothing. Not one to sit and rest, she was always busy. Even after a long day's work, Grandma would spend the evening cutting worn-out dresses, smocks, and shirts into scraps that would later become beautiful patchwork quilts.

Each quilt required many hours of work, and the designs, which appeared simple upon completion, were often quite complex. There seemed to be an infinite variety of quilt patterns, with names indicative of their design: pinwheel, fan, flower garden, star, log cabin, wedding ring, bow tie, nine patch, and Dresden plate were just a few favorites.

It took many nights to cut out the desired shapes. And it took many more, along with hundreds of tiny stitches, to hand-assemble the pieces into the desired pattern. Next the colorful shapes were sewn into a block and the blocks sewn together. Then an intricate border was designed, assembled, and stitched to the edge of the quilt. When the quilt top was finally completed, another pattern was chosen and traced onto the top. This was the pattern that the quilters would follow when they joined the top, filler, and backing. Each step required time, care, and craftsmanship. And all these many years later, the quilts remain a testimony to Grandma's artistry.

The joy she took in this task was evident, but I'm sure that quilt making was more than just a pleasant pastime for her. Created out of necessity, quilts brought comfort and warmth to her family. But for me today, they mean so much more—warming my heart as well as my toes. Hidden among the many tiny stitches, I find our family's history pieced together from thousands of tiny fabric scraps.

When I was growing up, many of these quilts adorned our beds. I used to lie stretched out on a quilt and make a game of looking at the patterns, letting my imagination explore the patches. A small swatch I'd recognize as one of Grandma's old smocks reminded me of her deep pockets that held treats of peppermints, butterscotch, or lemon drops. A bit of a red calico apron evoked thoughts of Grandma's kitchen with its sweet scents of cinnamon and ginger. A rectangle of lavender-flowered chintz recalled one of my mother's favorite housedresses and memories of her primping before my father arrived home from work.

But along with revisited memories, there are mysteries hidden in the quilt tops—souvenirs from garments worn long before I was born. I wish I knew their secrets too. Who once played with boyish glee in the sky-blue cowboy print? And which little girl danced in delight dressed in her favorite nursery rhyme—a gold print bearing "three little kittens and tiny mittens"? These secrets from the past are indelibly inscribed on

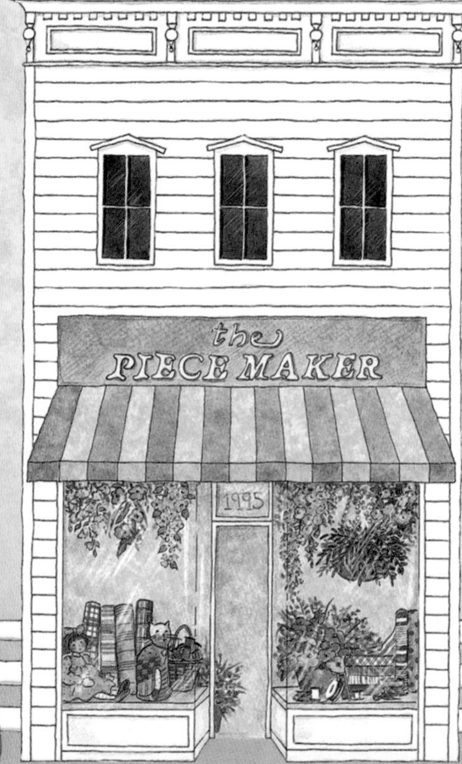

Grandma's quilts. As long as my family and I are good caretakers, we can preserve this delicate peek into the past.

Someday I will pass these quilts and stories on to my children, reminding them of the spiritual legacy handed down from their great-grandmother. I will teach them the truth of a saying I once read: "A quilt is a thing that endures because it reflects the soul of its maker." Along with her craftsmanship, Grandma's quilts reveal her patience, her love, and the value she placed on good stewardship—making the most of everything she had.

Life is a lot like the pattern of a patchwork quilt, having infinite possibilities for its design. But if our life is to reflect the soul of our Maker, then we need to allow him to assemble the pieces into his grand design—not ours.

Grandma left her life in the hand of the Master "piecemaker." And she taught her children and grandchildren to do the same. One of the passages Grandma liked to quote was: "You made all the delicate, inner parts of my body and knit me together in my mother's womb. . . . Your workmanship is marvelous. . . . Every day of my life was recorded in your book. . . . How precious are your thoughts about me, O God" (Ps. 139:13-17, NLT).

Besides creating beautiful quilts and reclaiming old houses, Grandma devoted her life to rescuing lost souls. She had a rare gift for seeing that even lives that have become tattered and torn can, with God's love, be remade into something beautiful. I know when Jesus said, "Blessed are the peacemakers: for they shall be called the children of God" (Matt. 5:9, KJV), he was referring to those who work for peace. But I think those words were meant for my grandmother, the *piecemaker,* too.

ABCDEFGHIJKLMNOPQRSTUV
WXYZ
Ask and it shall be given to you;
seek, and you shall find; knock,
and it shall be opened to you.
matthew 7:7
April
1993
allen Stouffer © 1993

Secrets of the Garden

Ask and it shall be given to you; seek, and you shall find; knock, and it shall be opened to you.
MATTHEW 7:7, NASB

It's spring, and the sweet smell of lilacs wafts through the open window, turning my thoughts to the summer I first learned about gardening. I was a newlywed, eager to transform my first house into a beautiful home. And I was in awe of my next-door neighbor Mary's magnificent garden. Ferns, hostas, daylilies, hydrangea, hollyhocks, columbine, roses, and impatiens burst from borders, tumbled from trellises, and crowded garden pathways. Garden benches, framed by pink, purple, and white blossoms, welcomed visitors and called them to linger.

Everyone said Mary had a green thumb, that she could poke a pumpkin seed into the ground and an entire pumpkin patch would spring up by morning. But Mary just laughed and said, "You can't have a garden without lots of hard work!"

And the truth was that from early morning until late evening I would see Mary weeding, watering, hoeing, planting, cutting, or spraying. "My garden is a work in progress—always changing, always growing. That's why I call it 'Never Done!'" she joked with me.

I loved to look into her yard, and I longed to have a garden just like Mary's. So I decided I would plant one. It couldn't be that hard.

My favorite flowers were, and still are, roses. Since I didn't know much about gardening, I thought perhaps I'd start with just a few dozen rose bushes. A trip to the nursery convinced me I was right. Lured by the brilliant fire of vivid red roses and the faint blush of pale peach blossoms, I found myself loading up a rainbow of rose bushes. I couldn't wait to get home with them and start transforming our yard.

Wooed by memories of June Cleaver and images from *Better Homes and Gardens,* I temporarily forgot about steamy Midwestern summers and my tendency to get sunburn and heatstroke.

My first inkling that I might have made a small mistake came when I unloaded the plants from the rusty old pickup I had borrowed from my uncle. By the time I'd finished unloading and carrying the roses to the backyard, I was exhausted, limp, and dehydrated. I was ready to lie in the shade with a tall glass of lemonade. But then I saw the quick movements and spry steps of my elderly neighbor in her garden, and I knew I couldn't be outdone.

Quickly I dug some holes and plopped the bushes into them. Then I stood back and admired my work. I was thrilled with the results. The plants, fresh from the nursery, looked spectacular. Perhaps I was destined to be a gardener after all.

In the weeks that followed, I admired my roses daily. But one by one the blooms began to fade. I noticed there were new shoots on the bushes, but they grew wild and long, and they weren't producing roses. Next I noticed that the leaves had begun to yellow, and on closer inspection I discovered they were covered with black spots. Soon the stalks were stripped of their leaves, and the bushes looked like a swarm of locusts had swept through. My garden looked pathetic—especially compared with Mary's.

All this time, Mary went on tending her expanding garden and never commented about my waning plot. Finally, one evening while crickets chirped and the sky darkened to a faint violet, Mary invited me over to rest on the back porch swing that overlooked her garden. After admiring her luxuriant plantings, I glanced over at my bare bushes. "Mary, I guess I just don't have your green thumb," I said, defeated.

"Ah," was all Mary said at first, nodding her head slightly.

"Where did I go wrong?" I asked, finally getting over my foolish pride.

"Roses take a lot of work," Mary told me. "There's more to a garden than just digging a hole and plunking something into the ground. If you want to have a garden—especially a rose garden—it takes lots of tending."

Then Mary patiently explained about roses—fertilizing the soil before planting to give a good foundation, pruning and deadheading blossoms to force more blooms. She talked about diseases, like black spot, that threaten roses and how important it is to see to the overall good health of the plants.

"Not even constant spraying will turn a sickly rose into a thriving one if the roses have to endure poor soil, lack of water, or too few nutrients," Mary said.

While lightning bugs flashed around us, Mary taught me the secrets of the garden.

By the time she finished, I was beginning to understand why Mary spent so much time gardening.

"I feel awful, Mary," I told her. "I spent a lot of money buying those roses, and now I have nothing to show for it!"

"Oh, I wouldn't say that," said Mary. "Looks like you've learned a lot, and perhaps you'd like to try again. But first, you might want to read up on roses." With that, Mary got up, went into the house, and returned with a lovely volume entitled *The Art of Roses.* That night I poured over glossy photos of exquisite blooms with names such as 'American Pride,' 'Gypsy,' and 'Razzle Dazzle.' By morning I had a new plan, and this time I decided to ask Mary to help me implement it.

"Mary, would you go with me to the nursery for more roses?" I asked. "I'd like to try again. And maybe this time you could help me with my choices."

By summer's end, I'd managed to plant and nurture a modest garden. With Mary's help, we planted new rose bushes along with enough perennials and annuals to flank a garden bench she'd rescued from her shed. In the front yard we planted marigolds that paraded in a cheery ring around the mailbox and marched straight up the walkway leading to the porch. It was a nice manageable plot, though it still required considerable tending.

As I spent hours laboring in my garden, it gave me the time and solitude to reflect on many things. I thought about Mary's advice on starting with a good foundation and her warning about seeing to the overall health of the plants. As I watered and weeded, fertilized and pruned, I discovered that the garden held analogies for life. I realized that all summer I'd been so busy with my new married life that I hadn't been spending much time on my spiritual life. My faith in God was my foundation, but I saw that if I wanted to be a beautiful flower in his garden, I needed to take better care of my spiritual health. I resolved to become more faithful in church attendance, Bible study, and prayer.

I grew a lot that summer. I learned that lives, like roses, need a lot of tending. And I finally understood the saying, "People, like plants, blossom in their gardens."

HEARTS TO READ WHAT HANDS HAVE WRITTEN
you are our letter,
written in our hearts
2 corinthians 3:2
1996
T.S. Elliot
NARNIA
C.S. Lewis
THOREAU
verse - wm. Stouffer
Ellen Stouffer 1994©

Written in Our Hearts

You are our letter, written in our hearts.
2 CORINTHIANS 3:2, NASB

It was hidden behind a row of neatly stacked shoes, tucked underneath a folded blanket in a darkened corner of the closet shelf. The colorful cover of the old cigar box immediately charmed us, and we were intrigued to find it secreted amid the other more practical necessities that graced our father's closet shelf. It was three weeks after my father's death, and my sister, Judy, and I were helping our mother by taking over the dreaded task of sorting through Daddy's belongings.

There was no doubt the old cigar box was his treasure box. Its contents bridged the worlds of boyhood and manhood. Nestled beneath its lid we found items a young boy would have cherished, including a gold pocket watch, miniature moccasins (a souvenir from Oklahoma), an ebony-handled pocketknife, a rock, and sketches of sailing ships drawn in his boyish hand.

Other contents were keepsakes from the 1930s—old postcards with scenes from his beloved Ozarks and faded sepia-toned photos of people unknown to us. But the most significant element of the cache was a packet of letters written in Mother's familiar hand. The first—postmarked October 31, 1933—was written just two weeks after our parents' elopement and before they revealed this secret to Mother's parents.

Judy and I shared a quick, excited glance, both of us understanding the significance of this find. Our mother, a fastidious housekeeper, was not one to save mementos from the past. Although we both had questioned her many times, it appeared that not a letter, journal, or scrapbook had escaped her penchant for cleanliness rather than sentimentality. But now we'd just uncovered a secret passageway into our parents' past.

Fearing the letters might upset our grieving mother, we secreted them away to be read at a later time. When we were finally able to steal away and read them, they introduced us to a mother and dad we had never known—a couple younger than we were at the time of this discovery. They revealed a teenage bride and spoke of her loneliness while apart from her new husband. They whispered words of love, and they shared hopes and dreams for the new life that our mother and dad were starting together. One especially dear missive expressed a longing for "just a small, cute house to call our own." This same letter offered encouragement to my dad as he searched for a job in the middle of the Depression.

Reading those sweet words more than forty years after they were penned, I was certain Daddy must have reread them many times. I know their message was written deeply within his heart.

My father's daughter, I too am a conservator of letters. I can't bear to throw away a letter from a friend or loved one, so I store letters and notes in shoeboxes, hatboxes, and drawers. I'm afraid I'm creating a housekeeping nightmare for my children upon my own demise, but perhaps they too will treasure this written history found in the letters of friends and kin.

The fact is, I love letters. For me there is nothing quite so pleasing as finding the familiar handwriting of a friend tucked amid credit card and phone bills and promotions suggesting I buy pizza or have my carpet cleaned. A friend's letter is like finding a precious gift in my mailbox. It is a continuing kindness I can enjoy again and again.

I'm concerned that letter writing is becoming a lost art. How will future generations find out about our everyday lives? I own numerous books that are collections of letters. Two of my favorite volumes contain letters of pioneer women, which give me a peek into the lives of the early western settlers. One letter from the late 1800s reads: "We began our journey of one thousand miles on foot with a handcart for each family. . . . There were in our tent my husband with one leg, two blind men . . . a man with one arm, and a widow with five children." And another: "Am wearing the Bloomer dresses now; find they are well-suited to a wild life like mine. Can bound over prairies like an antelope, and am not in so much danger of setting my clothes on fire while cooking when the prairie winds blow."

Even letters I've recently received contain a written history of sorts: "Margo's cousin is getting married. . . . Beth is 7½ months pregnant—a boy. . . . Arthur had a mild heart attack, but seems to be doing well now." And on a more spiritual note: "I am so amazed at how God directs our lives . . . I feel he has been preparing me for this new adventure for years."

It's not surprising that the Bible, the history of God's people, contains a collection of letters too. Many books of the New Testament were originally letters written to people in the early church, and their message is as relevant today as when they were first written. One of Paul's letters to the Ephesians says, "Follow God's example in everything you do. . . . Live a life filled with love for others, following the example of Christ, who loved you" (Eph. 5:1-2, NLT). His letters give us instruction, inspiration, and encouragement today, just as they did for their original recipients.

Some might say letters are unnecessary; we can look back and record our past. But a favorite author of mine, May Sarton, summed up a book of her letters by saying: "What I might write about the past could not have the freshness of a letter written forty years ago . . . [these letters] have given me back a self I had nearly forgotten. As an old woman I rejoice to find myself young again."

Part of what made the discovery of my parents' letters so wonderful was that similar sense of encountering Mother and Daddy in their youth. Without those letters I could never have imagined my mother at sixteen gushing, "Honey, I miss you so much. . . . Can you come back a day early, but don't tell Irish I asked you to. He'd tease me too much."

Both my parents have been gone for a long time now, yet their lives remain written in my heart. But some days the longing to talk with them is almost more than I can endure. On those days I pull out the old letters—those they wrote to me and the ones found in Daddy's treasure box—and I reread them, bringing my parents close to me once again. Someday I'll pass those letters along to my children—but I think I'll wait to let them discover their dad's and my love letters on their own. There is something delicious about feeling you are eavesdropping on the past.

ABCDEFGHIJKLMNOPQRSTUVWXYZ
In all ways acknowledge Him, and He shall direct thy path. Prov 3:6
allen Stouffer
© 1999

Plats, Paths, and Promises

In all thy ways acknowledge him, and he shall direct thy paths.
PROVERBS 3:6, KJV

The contents of a lifetime were strewn out over the lawn in front of the old farmhouse. I wandered around with the other auction-goers examining pieces of interest and searching for treasures among the stacks of "junk" boxes that rested all around. Then I spied a box of old books—and my heart quickened. An impassioned bibliophile, I'm always sure that somewhere, hidden amid dog-eared mysteries with names like *Tickled to Death* and *Something the Cat Dragged In,* there is a real pearl just waiting to be discovered.

While many types of old books call to me, I have a special ardor for journals written in shaky hands by lamplight and any book that spurs my imagination about people who lived long ago. Perhaps that's why a large, old volume caught my eye—a dark green leather tome that bore the title, *Combination Atlas Map of McHenry County, Illinois–1872.* At fourteen by seventeen inches, it stood out from the other volumes. And the remnants of a gold, embossed seal—showing maps, globes, and a surveyor's journal—still looked impressive, even after all these years.

When I opened the book, the yellowed pages revealed a beautifully illustrated plat book that displayed the farms and villages that lay along the Fox River. Faded lithographs illustrated houses, trees, wagons, buggies, horses and riders, grazing sheep and cattle—all depicting daily life in the last quarter of the nineteenth century. Farms revealed the harvesting of apples and the baling of hay, and one especially grand estate showed two ladies in bustled gowns and a gentleman in a waistcoat playing a game of croquet on the lawn. This estate was identified as the residence of Samuel Ackerman, section 5, Algonquin, township of McHenry County, Illinois.

I quickly scanned over the page, discovering the names of Algonquin's early settlers and their businesses, schools, and churches. But while I found these facts fascinating, what intrigued me most was

imagining the lives behind the sketches. I longed to discover the history of the Ackermans in order to learn more about their world. Who were they, and where did they come from? How did they decide to settle in Algonquin, and what led them to this particular farm? Were their lives as idyllic and simple as the quaint little drawings hinted, or were they difficult and wearisome?

For weeks after purchasing the plat book, I poured over the volume and searched the library for clues about these early founders, thinking that perhaps someday I might write a story about their lives. But even though I researched old newspapers and documents, I didn't discover any accounts of heroic deeds or evidence of fame. I could find neither letters nor living descendants to tell me what brought the Ackermans to the Fox River Valley, and nothing to reveal the essence of their days. Perhaps that's just as well, because now they may simply live on in my imagination. And fantasy is often much more fun than truth.

I imagine them having parties in the parlor, enlivened by a sassy, fiddle-playing farmer and a foot-tapping, banjo-playing blacksmith. In winter, I see them ice skating on the river and sleighing through the countryside. And in the summer, I see them feasting with relatives and friends at picnics and church socials along the banks of the Fox River.

Reason tells me that their lives also had hardships, but I prefer to think of them in an idyllic past. Living as I do in a frenzied and complex world, it relaxes me to think of their lives as simple and full of fun and ease.

Even though I haven't decided whether the book holds any material for my writing, I continue to enjoy looking at the lithographs and imagining the potential of each person's life. For a life that we perceive as ordinary may have great value in God's eyes.

I'd like my own life to count for something. But when I'm relying on myself, I'm often uncertain what to do. My perspective is limited. However, God's vantage point is more like that of the plat artist. I envision him looking down from heaven, surveying the hills and valleys of my life. And while I can see only what's in the foreground, God sees and knows all. That's why I'm glad he is the Master Architect and Designer of the "plat" for my life, and I'm grateful for his promise: " 'For I know the plans I have for you,' says the Lord. 'They are plans for good and not for disaster, to give you a future and a hope. In those days when you pray, I will listen' " (Jer. 29:11-12, NLT).

I don't know if God's plan means my name will be recorded in the history books or lost in the annals of time. Either way is fine, as long as I make the most of what God has given me. When the contents of my life are spilled before him, I hope he won't have to sort through a lot of junk without finding anything worthwhile. Like my discovery of the plat book, I hope he finds a treasure in me.

Each one has received a special
gift; employ it in serving one another.
1 Peter 4:10
Ellen Stouffer © 1988
March
1988

Quilting Bee

As each one has received a special gift, employ it in serving one another.

1 PETER 4:10, NASB

An old quilting frame often held pride of place in the middle of our family room. Since it could be unfurled to a size of seven feet by nine feet, it took up most of the room. When a quilt was ready to be finished, Daddy would help Mother roll the newly pieced quilt, layered with its batting and backing, onto the frame. Then they'd set chairs all around the perimeter so it was ready for the real work to begin.

Every Tuesday, shortly after their husbands had left for work and the last child had been sent off to school, my mother's friends would arrive for the quilting bee. By then a pot of homemade vegetable soup or a pan of chicken and dumplings was simmering on the stove, and the aroma of freshly baked bread filled the air. Soon the doorbell announced the arrival of Mother's church sewing circle.

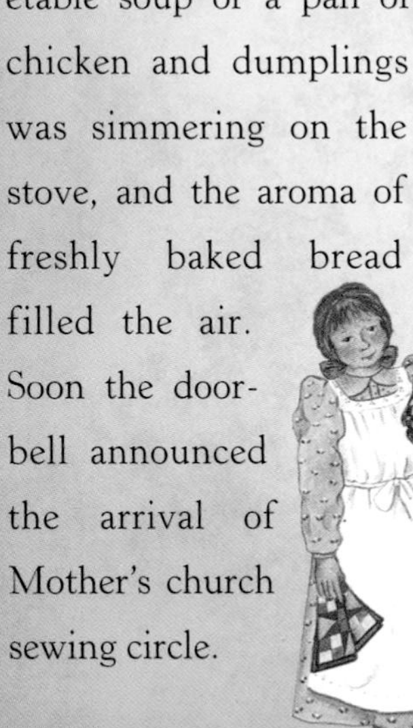

The women were as diverse as the many-hued fabrics that made up the patterns of the patchwork quilt. There was Polly Wainwright—kind, plump, and soft-spoken—whose generous mouth always curved into a quick smile at the sight of a child, a kitten, or a puppy. Polly had been the primary-class Sunday school teacher for the last twenty years, and all the children of the church adored her.

Helen Ackerman, a slim, energetic, no-nonsense woman, usually accompanied Polly. She was also a Sunday school teacher and another permanent fixture at the Baptist church.

Next there was Dorothy Rankin, thin, red-haired, and twittery. Her deft fingers were equally at home using needle and thread or pumping out hymns on the old organ. Alva Miller—prim and meticulously coiffed and dressed—always arrived precisely on time. Alva always saw to it that bouquets of flowers graced the front of the church on Sunday mornings.

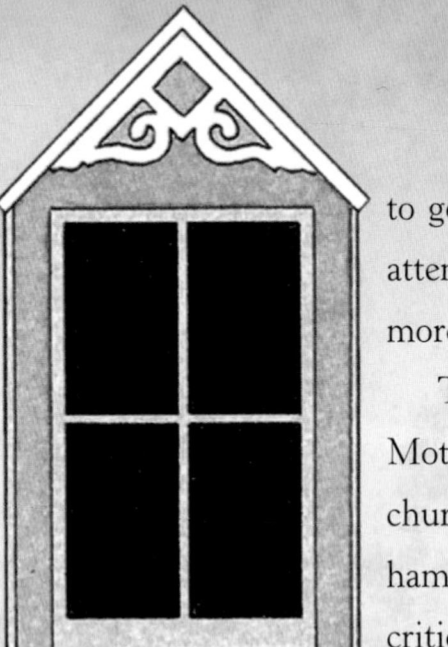

Bringing up the rear was Aileen Olson. She was tall and gaunt and had a hawkish, pinched nose that always looked as though she had just whiffed something offensive. She was prone to driving her church friends a little crazy with her incessant gossiping and faultfinding.

My mother's dearest friend, Evangeline Nagle, always came early to help get everything ready. A dark-haired beauty, as quiet and reserved as my mother was exuberant and friendly, she hovered in the background, hanging up coats and unobtrusively meeting anyone's slightest need.

Arriving in a chorus of happy greetings, the women sounded like some grand orchestra tuning up for the day's event. Presented with a welcoming cup of coffee, they eventually settled down to the business of the day—a quilting bee and lively conversation, the latter often seeming to be the first priority. They talked congenially of children and church, mending and baking, and the sale on dry goods at Miller's department store.

Aileen made sure everyone knew the latest tidbits: "Has everyone else been as shocked as I have at the way the new minister lets his children run unchecked through the sanctuary?" she would ask. Or she might comment, "Did you ever see anything quite as ridiculous as that flowered dress Maribelle Adams wore to church on Sunday? Why, it made her look as big as a house. And while I wouldn't want to be one to gossip . . ." At this point, everyone would smile and attempt not to laugh, knowing no one loved to carry tales more than Aileen Olson did.

Trying to keep the conversation more "Christian," Mother would steer the talk into the plans for the harvest church supper or suggest the women make some new gingham curtains to cheer up the church nursery. Although critical and gossipy, Aileen always responded to those types of suggestions by being the first to help with a donation.

All morning, as their needles darted in and out, the conversation flowed with a snappy, staccato beat. After a morning of sewing, my mother and Evangeline would get everything ready for the shared luncheon. After lunch, satisfied with good food and a morning of fellowship, the ladies would pack up their sewing things. Chirping cheery good-byes, they'd hurry home to finish a few chores, greet returning children, and prepare their family's supper.

Mother would tidy up and look over the day's work. Then, after supper, she would sit down and patiently begin ripping out the stitches Aileen Olson had made.

The first time I realized what was happening, I asked why she was doing that.

"Well, honey, Mrs. Olson's stitches are just too big and are carelessly done," Mother said. "But I'll fix them." And she started replacing the stitches in her own tiny, neat hand.

"If she sews so badly, why do you let her come?" I persisted.

Mother stopped her work and looked at me thoughtfully.

"Mrs. Olson is rather lonely, you know. She hasn't many friends."

"Of course not," I said, with all the assurance of a know-it-all nine-year-old. "She isn't very nice to anybody!"

But that kind of talk always met with a stern look and a warning from my mother: "When you talk like that, you become just like the person you're criticizing. God told us to love one another and pray for those who spitefully use us. So you just keep on being nice."

Each week the women would return, and Aileen would take up where she left off—stitching and complaining. And each week after Aileen left, my mother would spend hours ripping out and replacing the stitches. If Aileen ever realized my mother's kind deception, she never let on.

More than forty years have passed since the Baptist churchwomen gathered for quilting and conversation. All but Aileen and Evangeline have gone home to be with their heavenly Father. Evangeline continues to quietly serve and minister to her friends and neighbors. But many years ago Aileen's only daughter placed Aileen in a nursing home, finding it impossible to care for her mother and endure her constant bickering and complaining. Up until my mother passed away, she visited Aileen, bringing her cookies, conversation, and crossword puzzle books—doing anything she could to show a little kindness.

My mother, with her gift of giving and her thoughtful nature, formed much of my early understanding of how God expects us to love one another. She also taught me to see the gifts he conferred on others. She valued her friends and allowed each to use her talents in whatever way God had blessed her. Her good friend Evangeline once shared a letter from my mother. It was full of praise, admiration, and love for her dear friend.

"Your mother was so good at everything, and I always felt awkward and clumsy," Evangeline said, "but she made me feel like the most valuable person in the world."

I think my mother was right about Evangeline. I can still see her getting out china, handing out cups of coffee, pouring cream, and unobtrusively wiping up a spill—quietly ministering to her friends. And I remember Polly and Helen playing, laughing, and teaching children; Dorothy making the world smile with her music; Alva arranging flowers; and Aileen opening her generous purse.

I like to think about being reunited with my mother and her sweet friends in heaven. I'm assured that grace, acceptance, and love abound there. And I'm sure it's a place made even more beautiful by the presence of the women from the quilting bee.

ABCDEFGHIJKLMNOPQRSTUVWXYZ
BLESS THIS HOUSE
1992
NOEL
Love One Another
Faith Hope Love
Serve One Another
Through wisdom a house is built, and by understanding it is established, and by knowledge the rooms are filled with all precious and pleasant riches. Prov. 24:3,4
©1992

Where Love Abides

Through wisdom a house is built, and by understanding it is established;
by knowledge the rooms are filled with all precious and pleasant riches.

PROVERBS 24:3-4, NKJV

The wind blows, picking up handfuls of freshly fallen snow and swirling it across open cornfields laid bare to winter. Though it makes the drive more hazardous, I'm excited that we will have a white Christmas. In the Midwest, December sometimes can be moderate and dry.

This year it's only my husband and me packed into the front seat of our pickup truck—which we've chosen to drive rather than one of our cars because it holds more presents. There will be four generations of our clan traveling from Michigan, Wisconsin, and northern Illinois to assemble at the suburban St. Louis home of my husband's parents.

We sing, "Over the river and through the woods to grandmother's house we go . . ." just like we used to in the "old days" when our car was filled with the chatter of three squirming, giggly, and sometimes cranky children, who just couldn't wait to get to Grandma and Grandpa's house for the holidays.

I can't imagine a small, quiet Christmas because for both my husband and me, the holidays have always meant a large gathering of kin. And even though we changed houses and cities eleven times and lived in four different states over the course of our children's growing-up years, going "home for the holidays" has always been our family tradition.

Still, there were times when I wondered if those trips were worth all the effort. Preparing for them seemed as much work as planning for an expedition to Antarctica. Regardless of how many Christmas presents we were carrying, we needed plenty of room for a well-stocked travel kit. This meant packing up well-loved teddy bears, frizzy-haired Barbies, dog-eared copies of books such as *The Velveteen Rabbit* and *The Cat in the Hat,* dozens of Matchbox cars, crayons and coloring books, plus assorted treats, pillows, and blankets. I included anything I could think of to make the eleven-hour trip pass pleasantly and quickly. Yet despite this careful preparation,

we were scarcely out of the drive before we heard cries of, "Are we there yet?" Then came a chorus of, "He's touching me," followed by wails of, "She's on my side!"

Eager to ease the anxiety of car trips, my husband and I purchased a van in order to give our three children more room. I'd like to say this took care of the problem. It didn't. Somewhere between Kalamazoo and Chicago, two would gang up on one, and the bickering would continue until I suggested we play a game of "alphabet signs"—seeing who could be the first to find the entire alphabet on roadside billboards. When this grew old, we would break into funny camp songs and log a few more miles with "John Jacob Jingle Heimer Schmitt" or "There Was an Old Woman Who Swallowed a Fly."

That's what I remember. However, when our grown children got together with us recently and starting sharing their memories, my husband and I looked at each other in amazement and jokingly wondered if they had been on the same car trips!

Our children have forgotten all about those tiring hours trapped in the car with wiggly, complaining siblings. They no longer remember who stepped over the imaginary line that divided sides—or that they even had sides.

Instead, they remember all the good times that followed. They bask

in memories of huge dinners where four generations of family gathered for good food, conversation, and fun. They remember spending cold winter afternoons playing games like Monopoly and Clue with doting grandmas and grandpas, aunts, uncles, and a half-dozen cousins. Memories of fresh snowfalls include snow angels, giggles, snowball fights with dad and Uncle Nick, and careening down the hill on their sleds, cheered on by a flock of relatives.

And they recall Christmas as being the most special time of all—dinner at Grandma's, homemade cookies, presents, and reading the Christmas story out loud to the grown-ups.

Our children cherish those trips home, describing them as times of loving, laughing, understanding, helping, and working together—the real things that home and family are all about.

Though it may have taken a lot of time and work to give our children a sense of our family legacy, it was worth all the effort. They have grown up strong in character and secure in the knowledge that they are loved. And today they eagerly carry on the tradition, traveling many miles to bring their own families "home for the holidays." Henry Van Dyke, in "Home Song," probably said it best: ". . . every house where love abides and friendship is a guest, is surely home, for there the heart can rest."

Chocolate
Wm. Stouffer Wabash
LAKE SALAMONIE
CHIPPEWA
BEST
American Spinners
Mississinewa BAIT SHOP
HERBS
Monopoly
A friend loveth at all times.
Wabash Flyer
JOURNAL
LIFE
MATTHEW 6:21

Aunt Tillie's Attic

A friend loveth at all times.

PROVERBS 17:17, KJV

Attics are often dark, scary places where spiders hide and eerie shadows suggest things that go bump in the night. But at Aunt Tillie's house, the attic was a wonderland, a magical place to play, and a storehouse of family memories.

The first time I explored Aunt Tillie's attic, I was perhaps ten years old. It was summer, and I was thrilled to be spending a couple weeks with my cousin Stevie.

Usually when I visited, we weren't allowed to play in the upper part of the house because Aunt Tillie took in boarders and they lived upstairs. But this summer there were no tenants, so sometimes we played games in the empty rooms upstairs. On one of those days, I questioned Stevie about the door at the top of the stairs. He said it led to the attic. When I asked what was up there, he just shrugged and said he didn't know.

From then on I was intrigued, and I couldn't rest until I found out what was in the attic. One morning I asked Aunt Tillie if I could see it.

"Why would you want to do that?" she asked. "There's just a lot of old junk stored up there."

But I persisted and she said, "Okay. Wait for me to finish ironing this shirt, and I'll take you."

When she finished, I followed Aunt Tillie up the steep, narrow stairway that led to the attic. I don't know what I was expecting to see—ghosts, goblins, or a pirate's treasure chest—but what I found looked more like an antique store. Rolled-up rugs, old chairs, a grandfather clock, and other pieces of unused furniture crowded the edges of the space. A floor lamp without a shade, a rug beater, suitcases, toys, stacks of books, and several large steamer trunks filled

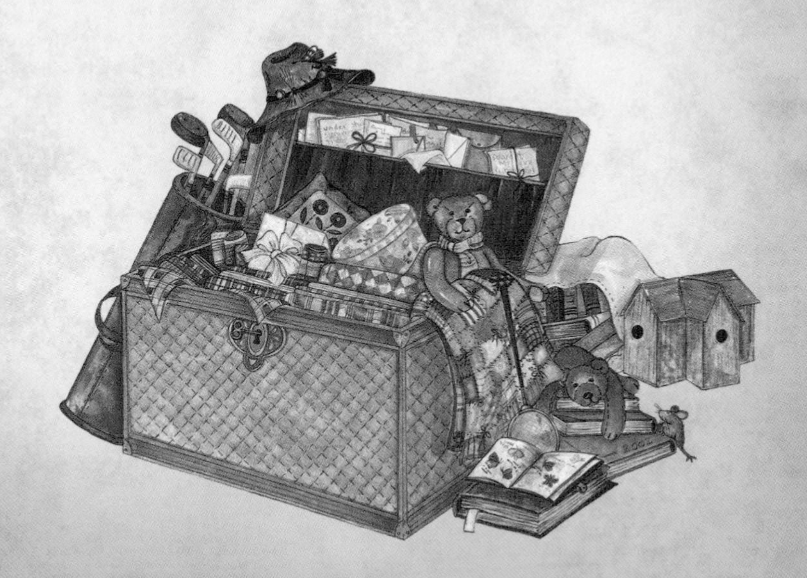

the center of the room.

Some light filtered in from the dormer window, but Aunt Tillie pulled a string that lit a bare bulb hanging from the ceiling. She looked around the attic in amazement at all the stuff accumulated there. "My, what a lot of memories we've put away up here," she said, sighing.

Before long we were deeply immersed in opening trunks and digging out treasures. We found photo albums, scrapbooks, old toys, and clothes. She let me try on old dresses, hats, jewelry, and high-button shoes.

Each new memento we unearthed elicited a story from Aunt Tillie. We laughed about an old record labeled *The Boogie Woogie Bugle Boy from Company B,* which prompted stories about my three youngest aunts, who loved to dance. We looked at black-and-white photos of my mother and aunts posed by vintage cars, and there were also photos of my two handsome uncles, who'd been killed in an accident before I was born.

Then we unearthed a scrapbook that contained copies of an old comic strip called "Tillie the Toiler." She told me this was where she had gotten her nickname, Tillie. Grandpa had started calling her that after she'd landed her first job, and she'd been called it ever since. That was the first time I heard her real name was Wilma.

The best part of the morning for Aunt Tillie came when we discovered her autograph album—a velvet-bound book filled with funny sayings: "Remember me when you are happy, keep for me one little spot, in the depth of thine affection, plant a sweet forget-me-not." That one was signed "Rose," and she had drawn a flower by her name.

Aunt Tillie smiled as she read the names of dear friends from her past, and she giggled like a young girl as she recalled some of their escapades.

By the time we finished looking at the photos and reading a few of the letters, the attic was growing hot, and Aunt Tillie said she suspected it was time for lunch. Red-faced and dust-smudged, we gathered up the keepsakes and carefully replaced them.

That was the first of many trips to explore the attic. Each one uncovered another forgotten memory, and I learned much of our family history up there. It was a sad day when we sorted through those memories for the last time. Aunt Tillie was moving to a different house in a neighboring town, and I had gone over to help her clean out the attic. By then I was grown with a young family of my own, and I took along my nine-year-old daughter, Jennifer, to share our last attic adventure.

Jennifer was looking through an old trunk when she discovered a packet containing a newspaper clipping, some photographs, and a bundle of letters. She recognized the photo from the newspaper right away.

"Why, that's Aunt Verda," she said, pointing to a picture of Aunt

Tillie's second-to-the-youngest sister.

We pulled out the clipping, and I began to read the story about Aunt Verda. "Some call her a kook. Some call her wonderful," the headline said. According to the newspaper account, Aunt Verda and a woman named Mary Kaye had been friends since they were young girls. They'd continued their friendship through letters as they had married, moved to different places with their husbands, and had children. Then Mary Kaye's oldest child, Billy, developed kidney disease. He needed a transplant, but no one in the family was a suitable donor and the chance of a nonfamily member being a match was slim. Aunt Verda loved her friend so much that she offered to donate one of her kidneys and, amazingly, was found to be an almost perfect match. Her unselfish act saved the life of her dear friend's child.

Aunt Tillie, Jennifer, and I took time out to read some of the letters the two friends had written over the years and to look at photos of Aunt Verda and Billy.

When the attic was finally cleaned out, Aunt Tillie and I took one last, wistful look at it. I was hoping Aunt Tillie would fill up the attic in her new house so the future generation would have a place to explore. And Aunt Tillie . . . well, I'm not sure what she was thinking. But judging from her smile, I suspect she was lost in memories of friendships.

I had discovered a lot of things in Aunt Tillie's attic over the years, but that day I learned what Jesus meant when he said, "The greatest love is shown when people lay down their lives for their friends" (John 15:13, NLT).

Billy is now a man with grown children of his own, and he is recorded in medical history books as the oldest surviving kidney transplant recipient. Aunt Verda and Aunt Tillie have gone home to a family reunion in heaven. I'll renew their friendship there someday. And I've taken over Aunt Tillie's place as a caretaker of people—and of things.

Perhaps that's why one of my favorite pastimes is antiquing. It's as close as you can come to exploring someone's attic and learning to cherish their memories.

I have taught thee in the way of wisdom; I have led thee in the right paths.
Proverbs 4:11
Wabash
Be Mine
1·2·3·4·5·6·7·8·9·10
SUNDAY
MONDAY
TUESDAY
WEDNESDAY
THURSDAY
FRIDAY
SATURDAY
ART
MUSIC
PE
SAVE OUR EARTH
STAR STUDENT
Nancy
Dan
Barb
Peg
D'Ann
Bill
Pam
Kelly
JoDee
WRITING
ART
ellen Stouffer ©1994

School Days

I have taught thee in the way of wisdom; I have led thee in right paths.
PROVERBS 4:11, KJV

On a chilly, misty Saturday afternoon, I was searching through my collection of books for an old classic I wanted to reread when I found myself leafing through some of my childhood favorites. I glanced through *Anne of Green Gables, The Borrowers,* and *Black Beauty* before coming upon a cherished volume of *Little Women,* which I had won in a fourth-grade reading contest. Before long I was lost in the wondrous tale of "four sisters, who sat knitting away in the twilight, while the December snow fell quietly without, and the fire crackled cheerfully within," and I soon forgot about the volume I had gone to seek. Instead, I poured a cup of tea, lit my own fire, and set out on a familiar journey with Meg, Jo, Amy, and Beth—the four protagonists of Louisa May Alcott's classic tale.

It seems as if I have always gone traveling through the pages of books, but my real adventure with reading began in the fourth grade. My guide was a wonderful teacher named Miss Barker. While she approached all subjects with vitality and sparkle, her face lit up and she became particularly animated whenever she read to us or discussed her favorite books.

To motivate us to read, Miss Barker instituted a reading contest. For each book we read and reported on, she awarded us a prize. These prizes were small things children enjoyed: bookmarks illustrated with characters from children's books and nursery rhymes, colored pencils, playful stickers, and small pads of brightly colored paper. At the end of the year a special prize—a trophy and a beautifully illustrated volume of *Little Women* or *Treasure Island* (the winner's choice)—would be awarded to the child who had read the most books. I was determined to win that prize—and I did.

Every Wednesday the bookmobile came, and we checked out books. At first Miss Barker helped us with our selections by pointing out books she thought we might enjoy. She introduced me to a series of easy-to-read biographies, which recorded the outstanding deeds of famous people. One of my favorites was the story of Clara Barton, a Civil War nurse who founded the American Red Cross. I was surprised and delighted to discover that women could accomplish such great things. This inspired me to learn more, and soon I had gobbled up all the books in the biography series. From there I moved on to classic stories, such as *Heidi* and *The Swiss Family Robinson,* and current children's fiction, such as *Five Little Peppers and How They Grew.*

Once I had discovered that I could learn anything and go anywhere through books, I was completely captivated. Most days after school I could be found curled up with a book in a corner at home, lost in the adventures of real and imaginary characters.

I'm sure Miss Barker wasn't surprised when my newfound interest in reading transformed me from an average student to an excellent one. As my reading skills grew, so did my vocabulary and my ability to express myself on paper. My love of learning flowered as I developed a real curiosity about the world.

My interest in biographies led me to historical novels, in which the characters from history textbooks came alive. I found myself loving history—something I'd had little interest in before. I especially enjoyed accounts as seen through a woman's eyes, and I learned about our presidents by reading stories told from the viewpoint of Mary Todd Lincoln, Martha Washington, and Dolley Madison.

Geography changed from dull to exciting when I read adventure stories and poems about Tarzan, Gunga Din, and Hans Brinker with his silver skates. I took a riverboat ride and explored *Life on the Mississippi* with Mark Twain, and I saw New York from Betty Smith's vantage point in *A Tree Grows in Brooklyn.*

Not all of my lessons came from books, though. The Golden Rule—to treat others as we want to be treated—was at the top of the rule book for Miss Barker's classroom. She taught us lessons in honesty, courage, love, and perseverance, and she nurtured our pride in our country and its flag. And Miss Barker showed great patience, even on the most exasperating days, when she was constantly reminding Billy to put his hat in the cloakroom and tidy up his desk or dealing with Teddy, who often got into a fight with someone on the playground. She dealt with those infractions firmly but kindly, managing to convey the message that she still liked the child even though his or her actions displeased her.

Under Miss Barker's tutelage and tender care,

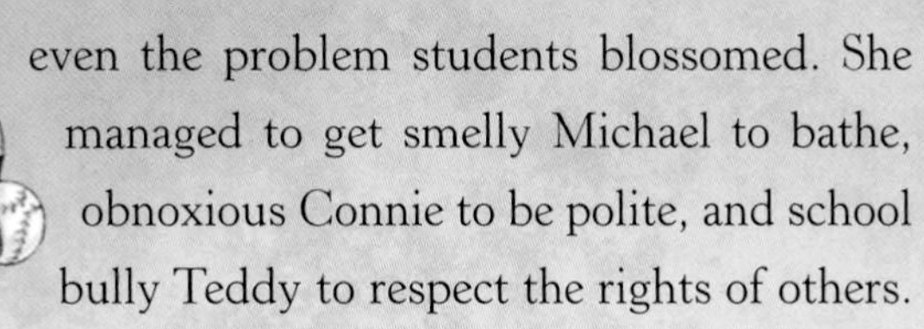

even the problem students blossomed. She managed to get smelly Michael to bathe, obnoxious Connie to be polite, and school bully Teddy to respect the rights of others. And then there were those, like me, who had just been ambling along before she instilled in us a zeal for learning. She taught us to read, write, and research—skills that equipped many of us to excel later in school and in life.

Rudyard Kipling once said, "He who can reach a child's heart can reach the world's heart." Through the children in her care, Miss Barker touched the world. Her students became doctors, attorneys, inventors, and teachers. I continued my love affair with books and became a writer and an editor. All of us benefited from her love and care.

My "thank you" to Miss Barker could easily come from the pages of my favorite *Little Women*. At the end of the story, Mrs. March—or "Marmee," as her daughters call her—tells her budding writer, Jo, "I think your harvest will be a good one." And Jo answers, "Not half so good as yours. . . . We never can thank you enough for the patient sowing and reaping you have done."

Give us this day
Sug
JAMS
A is for Ani my friend
We have this treasure in earthen vessels, that the surpassing greatness of power may be of God and not from ourselves 2 Cor 4:7
ellen Stouffer © 1995

Cakewalk Tea Party

We have this treasure in earthen vessels, that the surpassing greatness of the power may be of God and not from ourselves.
2 CORINTHIANS 4:7, NASB

For more than forty years Miss Alice had been a home economics teacher. By the time I knew her she had been retired for several years, but she volunteered as one of our 4-H club leaders. She was eager to help us learn the "home arts"—sewing, cooking, and entertaining. To help us with this task, Miss Alice proposed that we host an old-fashioned cake-walk tea party for our mothers.

I had never heard of a cakewalk tea. Miss Alice explained that each of us would be given a special cake recipe to bake and bring to the party. On the day of the party, each cake would be assigned a number and placed on a beautifully appointed tea table. The game was played a bit like musical chairs. As the music played, our mothers would stroll around a circle of numbered squares. When it stopped, they would land on a square. Miss Alice would draw a number, and the person standing on that square would win the cake with the corresponding number. Then the music would begin again, and the walkers would continue until everyone had won a cake.

The party was to be a dress-up affair, an idea that I loved. At twelve years old I envisioned myself as quite grown-up. The thought of entertaining my mother, an accomplished hostess, at an elegant tea party sounded wonderful to me.

Although Miss Alice offered to host the party at her home, each club member was expected to serve and act as a hostess. A few members were needed to help decorate and set up for the party, and I volunteered.

I had never been to Miss Alice's house, a pretty Victorian in an older part of town. As I approached her quaint and charming home on the day of the party, I thought it looked as though it belonged in an old movie. Inside, faded pale-pink wallpaper, adorned with cabbage roses, graced the dining-room walls. Dark moldings and gingerbread fretwork separated the dining room from the entry hall. It was the perfect setting for an old-fashioned party.

We quickly set about preparing for the cakewalk tea. Some of the girls were assigned to cover the tables with the crisp linen tablecloths that had been laid out. Miss Alice asked me to help her get out the teacups we would use for the party. As we took them from the china cabinet, Miss Alice told me she'd been collecting teacups for many years. I *oohed* and *aahed* at the dainty cups and saucers—some made of porcelain so fine they were almost transparent. I had never seen so many beautiful china patterns, many of which Miss Alice said were manufactured by Spode, Staffordshire, and Wedgwood. Some of the teacups were edged in gold plate, and others had surfaces that gleamed like satin. My favorite teacup had a yellow background and was densely covered with rosebuds. Miss Alice said this was called "chintzware" and, indeed, it looked like a piece of chintz fabric. As I handled the beautiful china, I dreamed of having such lovely things to use in my own home someday.

After getting out the teacups, I helped Miss Alice set out sterling-silver serving pieces, candelabra, and an exquisite tea set. Then Miss Alice let us cut flowers from her garden, and she showed us how to arrange them beautifully in vases. When everything was finished, I thought I'd never seen anything so exquisite in my life.

The party awed everyone. Even girls who were normally a bit rowdy seemed to speak in whispers when surrounded by gleaming candlelight, porcelain, and silver. Our mothers applauded our efforts and said we were wonderful hostesses. When the party ended, I vowed that when I grew up, this was precisely how I would entertain.

Miss Alice must have seen how much I enjoyed her lovely things, for she invited me to come to tea several times after that. During each visit she entertained me as if I were a grown-up and told me stories about the various pieces of china—where she had collected them, who had manufactured them, the country of origin, and the name of the pattern.

One of the more fanciful stories she told me concerned a delicate, blue-and-white willowware teapot, decorated with a printed pattern featuring a large willow tree by a little bridge and a pagoda. Two graceful little doves were kissing in the sky above. According to one legend, Miss Alice told me, the doves represented two Chinese lovers who had tried to run away together to escape an arranged marriage. Although they were pursued and killed, they were turned into doves so that they could stay together forever in the air. I knew this story was just a legend, but I thought it a most romantic one. I loved to look at the winsome doves and imagine the Chinese couple who gave up their lives for love.

I have always valued my friendship with Miss Alice. When I think of it now, I find it quite remarkable that she took such an interest in me as a child. Perhaps it was my eagerness to learn and my obvious love of the things she cherished.

I once asked Miss Alice if she used her fine china every day. She just laughed and said, "Oh, no. I have everyday dishes too."

"But wouldn't you like to use your china every day?"

Miss Alice just smiled thoughtfully and said, "A woman needs an everyday dish or two in her life!"

At the time I thought this a very curious answer. But Miss Alice was a bit eccentric, and I chalked it up to that. Looking back, however, I think her remark was more insightful than I had given her credit for. Many times Miss Alice had reminded me that fine china, though lovely, is very fragile. With each use, it requires special handling and care. Everyday dishes are more sturdy and practical—easier to use and less worry.

Sometimes I've wished that I'd been created more like a piece of fine porcelain—beautiful, elegant, and flawless—and less like an everyday dish. That used to trouble me a lot in my youth, for I aspired to be as talented as a famous artisan, as intelligent as a great scholar, and as beautiful as a movie star. But I've come to understand that I am beautiful because God lives within me. And though he may not have created me to be fine china, he can accomplish his will even through simple pottery. So these days I worry a lot less about my imperfections than I used to. And I'm glad that Miss Alice taught me not only to appreciate fine china, but to be grateful for everyday dishes too.

ABCDEFGHIJKLMNOPQRSTUVWXYZ
Come to me all who are weary and heavy-laden, and I will give you rest.
Matthew 11:28
Thou wilt keep him in perfect peace, whose mind is stayed on thee.
Isaiah 26:3
WABASH
Oct 1992
Ellen Stouffer © 1992

Bringing in the Sheaves

Thou wilt keep him in perfect peace, whose mind is stayed on thee.

ISAIAH 26:3, KJV

Bringing in the sheaves, Bringing in the sheaves
We shall come rejoicing, Bringing in the sheaves

Long before I had any idea what "sheaves" were, I was singing about them with gusto. At the church where I spent Sunday mornings and evenings and Wednesday nights, we were very fond of hymns. Occasionally an entire Sunday evening service was devoted to a "hymn sing"—an evening of music where everyone had a chance to choose their favorite hymns. "Page 23, 'Shall We Gather at the River,'" someone would call out. Then the organist would launch into an introduction, and everyone would join in the singing.

Brother Boone, an elderly man who always sat in the second row, was sure to choose the toe-tapping favorite, "Give Me That Old Time Religion." In his Kentucky backwoods vernacular this sounded like, "Gimme That Ol' Time Religion." Since I was too young to read and sang all of these songs from memory, I belted out this hymn just as Brother Boone sang it—though I wondered what "Gimme" was.

Brother Boone both frightened and fascinated me. He was a big mountain of a man who was rumored to be illiterate and to have worked as a lumberjack. Both rumors intrigued me, since I didn't know any adult who couldn't read or write—or any adult who was a lumberjack, for that matter. The people I knew all made their living in the steel mills or on the surrounding farms. As anyone will tell you who has ever traveled from Chicago through Bloomington, on to Springfield, and across to where the Mississippi River separates Illinois from Missouri, that part of the country is long on cornfields but short on trees. I'm not sure what brought Brother Boone to our town.

Despite his interesting history, Brother Boone's real claim to fame was that he was the best "Amener" I'd ever heard. He showed his fervor for God by frequently interrupting the song service or the pastor's sermon by shout-

ing in a thunderous voice, "Amen!" or "Hallelujah!" or "Praise the Lord!" His deep, rumbling voice expelled these words with such enthusiasm, in an otherwise quiet church, that the children usually giggled—although a stern warning look from Daddy encouraged me to muffle my giggles with my hands.

When I thought he wasn't looking, I often stared at Brother Boone and wondered about him. But he was far from my mind the autumn our church took an outing to Pere Marquette State Park in Grafton, Illinois. About an hour from my hometown, the park overlooks the confluence of the Mississippi and Illinois Rivers and is especially beautiful when the fall colors are at their peak. The members of our congregation went there for a shared picnic—our last before the weather became too cold to enjoy being outdoors.

My sister, Judy, and some of her friends were going to hike one of the trails, and I begged to come along. Judy reluctantly agreed but told me not to pester them. I was happy just to trail along in their wake.

Judy and her friends were laughing and giggling, and I was looking around when I suddenly sensed someone looking at me. I turned my head, and there was a beautiful doe standing statuelike in the forest—close enough that I could have reached out my arm and touched her. Her soft brown eyes stared straight into mine. I was mesmerized. I had loved deer ever since I'd been to see the movie *Bambi,* and this one looked exactly like Bambi's mother. We stood unmoving for a long time. Then she turned and bounded into the forest. I followed, trying to catch sight of her again, but she had disappeared. I tried to return to the path but got confused and couldn't find the trail.

Suddenly I realized my sister and her friends were nowhere in sight, and I couldn't hear the sound of their voices. I was terrified and called out in a shaky voice, "Ju-Juudy." When there was no answer, I started to cry, "Judy, Judy, Judy!" Then I heard footsteps coming through the trees. I thought Judy had heard and was coming to rescue me, but instead I discovered Brother Boone coming toward me. Now I started to cry in earnest. I was alone in the woods with this gruff giant of a man.

He knelt down in front of me and began talking quietly. He didn't sound at all like the shouting Brother Boone. In fact, for the first time I noticed his gentle Appalachian drawl. "It's okay, honey," he assured me. "You're not alone. I'm here now." He dried my tears with his hanky and took my small hand in his huge, calloused one. "You don't have to be afraid. We're gonna find your sister," he assured me. "If she's discovered that she's lost you, she's gonna be as skeered as you."

His hand was big and strong—like my daddy's. He led me back to the main path and over to a big boulder, where we sat down. "I think it's best if we wait here," he said. "I'm not sure which way your sister went, but I reckon when she discovers you're a-missin', she'll double back."

He asked me how I got lost, and I told him all about the deer. Then he started telling me stories of his own. He said Pere Marquette was home to lots of "critters," and if we watched, we might see pheasants or even a wild turkey. He also told stories about the Indians who once lived there and about the legend of the Piasa bird—a gigantic creature that lived thousands of years ago. I had seen the painting of the Piasa on the cliff that overlooked the river, and I was captivated by Brother Boone's story of the heroic Indian chief who risked his life to kill the great bird. I was so caught up in his tale that I was almost sad when Judy and her friends came running up.

First Judy hugged me, then she started fussing at me for wandering off and scaring them all half to death. But before she could say too much, Brother Boone said I'd had enough of a scare that I didn't need a scolding, too. Judy nodded meekly and said, "Yes, sir."

After that I didn't find Brother Boone frightening, though I still grinned when he began to shout in church. I noted the peace that came over his face as he sang, "What a Friend We Have in Jesus." Other times, I'd hear his deep, slightly off-key baritone sing with great passion, "We shall come rejoicing, bringing in the sheaves."

When I grew older and learned about the process of harvesting wheat—gathering the sheaves into the barn, separating the straw from the husk, and then winnowing the chaff from the grain—I finally understood why Brother Boone looked so peaceful as he sang. All his life he'd had to labor hard, but now he was resting in God's arms. And just as farmers separate the chaff from the grain, Brother Boone had cast out the worthless things of the world and focused his life on the heavenly truths of God. That big, illiterate backwoodsman was more learned than many a more formally educated man.

Today in our church we sing more praise songs than old hymns. But often the words of those hymns come back to me, and I sing their beautiful messages in my heart. They never fail to comfort me and make me feel closer to God. And I can close my eyes and envision Brother Boone up in heaven, tapping his heavy boots, clapping his big, bear-paw hands, and singing, "Gimme that ol' time religion. It's good enough for me!"

ABCDEFGHIJKLMNOPQRSTUVWXYZ
In wisdom
hast thou made
them all
Psalm 104:24
PLURIBUS
UNUM
4-H
Ellen Stouffer ©1993

The Carousel

In wisdom hast thou made them all.
PSALM 104:24, KJV

The day had finally arrived! After a two-hour car trip and one stop to top off the gas tank and have an ice-cold bottle of Coca-Cola, we were almost there. We waited our turn in the long line of used Fords, Chevys, dusty pickup trucks, and campers—all headed into the yawning parking lot of the Duquoin State Fair.

For weeks we'd been talking about this family outing. It was my first trip to the fair, and my excitement bubbled over like a teapot kept too long on a hot burner. Grandpa drove his big, boxy 1952 DeSoto. He and Uncle Johnny hardly said a word for the last hour. They couldn't wait to escape the confines of the car, where Aunt Tillie and Grandma had been talking animatedly for hours, and my cousin Stevie and I had taken turns every fifteen minutes uttering that universal children's phrase: "Are we there yet?"

In the car behind us were Mother and Daddy, my sister, Judy, and my cousin Connie. Stevie and I, at ages six and a half and seven, respectively, weren't allowed to wander around on our own, so we'd spend the day tagging along after Judy and Connie, who were in their early teens.

As soon as we rolled to a stop in the parking lot, the car doors sprang open and our excited voices called out where we were going and who was going with whom. The adults synchronized their watches, setting times and places to meet up again. The men headed first to see the farm equipment—huge tractors and harvesters. Aunt Tillie, Mother, and Grandma headed for the pavilion to see who had won the blue ribbon for the best apple butter, quilt, and other handmade goods. The four of us kids were off and running for the midway. We could already see the top of the tall Ferris wheel through the trees.

The midway was a jumble of sights, sounds, and smells. I liked the smells best. It was going to be an eating bonanza—cotton candy, fun-

nel cakes, sausage sandwiches, corn dogs, and popcorn. And as the day grew hotter there would be time for cherry snow cones and freshly squeezed lemonade.

Stevie and I were wide-eyed as we viewed a poster of "The World's Most Gigantic Snake." According to the poster's sensationalist claims, the snake was from a remote part of Africa—and it looked as though it could swallow a small village. We begged Judy and Connie to let us go see it. They affected a mature boredom but were actually happy to go along, although they had to feign indifference in order to appear "cool."

We entered the darkened tent, hearts pounding, sure we were about to view a snake rivaling the size and ferocity of Godzilla. What we found was an old, lazy boa constrictor that was too lethargic to wiggle.

We were easy prey for the shrewd carnival folks. Barkers called out to us, "Step right up, try your luck". . . at the ring toss, shooting ducks, dunking the man in the barrel, and an assortment of other games that lured us with promises of wonderful prizes. All the games were set up so it was almost impossible to win, but we were too young to know that. We still had fun trying our luck.

The highlight of the day for me was when, drawn as if by a pied piper, I followed the sound of the calliope to the shade of a pavilion. There I discovered a magnificent sight: a huge, whirling carousel. Rows of intricately carved flying horses, roosters, rabbits, giraffes, and other animals circled around and danced up and down in front of me. Each animal was beautifully designed and seemed to have a personality all its own. Like Alice discovering Wonderland, I was immediately drawn to a prancing white rabbit. Stevie chose a rearing stallion—he was in his cowboy stage. Judy and Connie acted nonchalant, but they agreed to ride "just to keep us happy." Judy hopped on the back of a colorful rooster, and Connie went for a long-necked giraffe.

Brass rings hung from the ceiling of the carousel, and the attendant who lifted me onto the rabbit said I could win another ride if I was able to grab one of them. Then the music of the calliope started to swell and the carousel began to turn. Round and round we went, up and down, gaining momentum. At first I hung on tightly, concerned I might slip off, but after a bit I dared to grab for one of the brass rings, even though I kept missing it. Judy turned and waved to me. I laughed and waved back. As soon as the carousel stopped, Stevie and I asked in unison, "Can we have another ride?"

But it was time to meet the rest of our family at the fish-fry tent. Later we saw the variety show. Then, long before we reached home, Stevie and I fell into a contented sleep in the backseat of Grandpa's car. I went to the fair many more times after that, but none rivaled the excitement of my first trip to the state fair.

Although I'm grown now, I continue to love the carousel, and I've become interested in its history and its art. I'd love to own an original carousel figure—but today a museum-quality hand-carved carousel animal can come with a price tag exceeding $100,000. Later carousel animals were mass-produced from aluminum and fiberglass and have far less value.

I learned that the best wooden carousel figures were created from the mid-1800s through the early 1900s, when there were more than five thousand carousels in America. The figures were made in cabinet shops, where master carvers whittled and chiseled fanciful animals with elaborate trappings that delighted children and grown-ups alike. Apprentices sometimes shaped the bodies following the master's design, but the master carver himself always carved the expressive faces. That's what makes these pieces so valuable—the touch of the master's hand made all the difference.

When I consider this, I see a parallel with our own lives. As human beings, we have a choice about how our life will be shaped. Will it end up having little worth, or will it become a valuable treasure? Will we let the world shape us, or will we allow ourselves to be touched by the Master's hand? "For we are God's masterpiece. He has created us anew in Christ Jesus, so that we can do the good things he planned for us long ago" (Eph. 2:10, NLT).

In this life, we only go around once. I want my life to be worth all that God can make it.

Feb
1987
now may our Lord who loved us, comfort and strengthen your hearts in every good work and word.
2 Thessalonians 2:17

Cut from the Same Cloth

Now may our Lord . . . who has loved us . . . , comfort and strengthen your hearts in every good work and word.

2 THESSALONIANS 2:16-17, NASB

My sister is the family genealogist, a fact I view with great pride and gratitude. I see her role as part historian, part conservator, and part caretaker—and I can always count on her to know when certain family events took place. She's meticulous about her research, and she never accepts hearsay as truth. Instead, she documents our lineage by giving us copies of preserved newspaper clippings, birth announcements, wills, and records from old family Bibles.

But my sister is interested in more than just constructing a long list of names on a family tree. She cares about the lives of our ancestors and searches for clues that will tell us who they were and how they lived. She is carefully compiling these facts and records into notebooks that can be handed down to future generations—a family history book.

I'm interested in family history too. And while I value the importance of my sister's work, I seek out family lore and legend. I see my role as storyteller, interpreter of facts, and keeper of dreams. That's why I was excited when my sister passed along the poem, "Her Quilt," written by my grandmother about her mother. I knew nothing about my great-grandmother other than facts such as the dates she was born, married, and died. Although I have a sepia-toned photograph of her and my great-grandfather, in it she looks severe and unsmiling. She has on a starched white shirt, and her hair is pulled back so tightly in a bun that I am often asked who the two men in the photo are. I tell them Grandpa's the one with the beard.

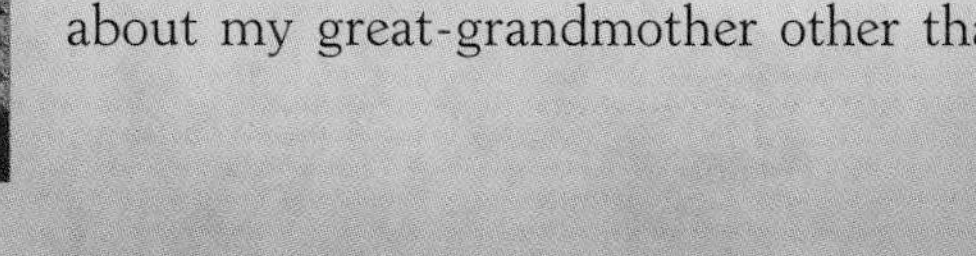

After reading my grandmother's poem, I now have another picture of Great-Grandma Jenkins. And, perhaps not surprisingly, I now see her as I've often seen my grandmother, my mother, and my sister—sitting when "evening shadows began to lengthen," a scrap bag beside her, cutting squares of cloth for a quilt. In her poem about her mother, my grandmother has drawn a portrait of a loving woman, one with concern for her friends and her family. She is a woman who loves, who prays, who blesses, who dreams—a woman like my grandmother, my mother, her sisters, my cousins, my sister, and, I hope, me. From my new perspective, I can see that the women of our family are all cut from the same cloth.

Like looking through a photograph album, in my memory I can see snapshots of these women: Grandma canning fruits and vegetables and giving them away to friends and

those in need; Mother spending the night at the hospital, sitting with a friend whose husband is dying; my sister heading up a food drive and delivering bags of groceries to needy families; my cousin off in a foreign country as a missionary sharing the word of God's love. I hear echoes of family voices singing hymns, uttering prayers, and reading stories and Bible verses to their children. I see a legacy of women of faith living their lives like the virtuous woman talked about in the Bible: "She is energetic and strong, a hard worker. She watches for bargains; her lights burn late into the night. Her hands are busy spinning thread, her fingers twisting fiber. She extends a helping hand to the poor and opens her arms to the needy. She has no fear of winter for her household because all of them have warm clothes. She quilts her own bedspreads. . . . She is clothed with strength and dignity. . . . When she speaks, her words are wise, and kindness is the rule when she gives instructions. She carefully watches all that goes on in her

household and does not have to bear the consequences of laziness. . . . Charm is deceptive, and beauty does not last; but a woman who fears the Lord will be greatly praised" (Prov. 31:17-30, NLT).

If it were not for the gift of my grandmother's poem, my great-grandma would have remained in my mind the stern woman in the photograph rather than the kind, prayerful woman who has now come to life for me. That's another legacy handed down from my grandmother—the knowledge that words, like works, can comfort and strengthen hearts.

The history of the women in our family is like a rich tapestry, woven with virtuous lives, good works, and wise words—a legacy my sister and I are thankful to pass along to our children. I hope that they, like those before them, will sew many a seam with "love, prayers, and blessings, together with dreams."

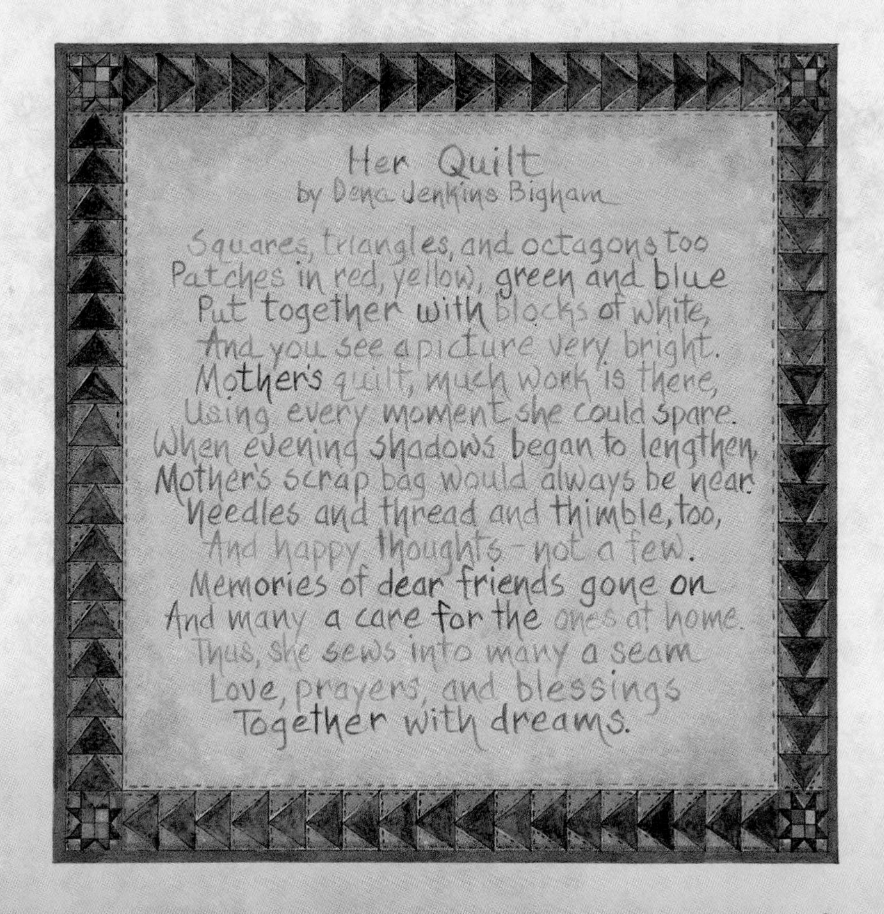

ABCDEFGHIJKLMNOPQRSTUVWXYZ
For where your treasure is, there will your heart be also.
Matthew 6:21
FRIENDSHIP
allen Stouffer © 1998

Forever Friends

For where your treasure is, there will your heart be also.
MATTHEW 6:21, KJV

The window is open, and down the block I hear an oldies radio station playing. The voices of the Everly Brothers sweetly harmonize to "Tonight You Belong to Me."

I'm trying to write, but, just like ants to a picnic, my thoughts keep returning to a grade-school gymnasium—where the melody continues but the childish voices of two young girls render a singsong imitation of the Everly Brothers' duo. The girls echo back to one another: "But tonight, you beloooooong to me. Just to little ol' me."

They are two sixth graders with their hair pulled back into bouncy ponytails. Both have dark hair, though one's hair has a hint of red and the other's is coal black. One wears saddle shoes with her bobby sox, the other wears penny loafers. Other than that, they are dressed alike in white angora sweaters and circular felt skirts adorned with poodles. I am one of the little girls—the one with the auburn hair. My best friend, Eleanor, is the other. Inseparable since we met, on this day we are practicing for the school's talent contest—an event, we assure each other, we are certain to win.

Our teacher listens to our recital and then suggests we sing something more "age appropriate," like "School Days." We are too well brought up to be disrespectful to our teacher, so we smile and nod in agreement. But when she walks away, we roll our eyes at each other, then have to look away to suppress our giggles. We think we are far too mature to sing baby songs like "School Days."

Eleanor and I met in the fourth grade when she sat at the desk next to mine. We never seemed to run out of things to say to each other. We talked about everything—about being taller than all the boys in class, not being allowed to stay up as late as our big sisters, and how we might get on the Mickey Mouse Club. I assured Eleanor she was prettier than Annette Funicello, and she told me I could sing better. We liked all the same things, laughed at the same jokes, and dreamed the same dreams.

Our backgrounds, however, couldn't have been more different. Eleanor's family was the only Jewish family that lived in our small

town. My family was Protestant, as were most of the other families who lived in the area. Her dad owned his own business. My dad worked in the steel mills, as did most of the other fathers in our town. Her family was more prosperous than most of the people in our community, but that didn't mean anything to Eleanor and me.

When we weren't together, we spent as much time on the phone as our parents would allow. We wrote notes several times a day and passed them back and forth at school or hid them in our secret spot—the rotted-out hollow of an old tree.

Every weekend we begged to spend Friday night at each other's house. We'd take turns hosting "slumber" parties—where we'd do everything but sleep. We painted our toenails, secretly tried on our sisters' makeup, and laughed hysterically at each other's jokes. Our favorite meal was pizza. We were "in love" with Elvis, though neither set of parents approved of him. The only fan mail I ever wrote was our joint letter asking for his autograph.

We also dreamed about what we'd do one day. We planned to marry and decided each of us would have five girls—who would be best friends, just like us. We made up names for ourselves: she was Lauren and I was Lisa. We were sure these would be the names of our firstborn daughters. We pledged that we'd be friends forever.

Junior high brought some separation into our lives, since we no longer had all the same classes. But we still passed notes in the halls. Friday night became movie night, when we'd get together with the other girls who were becoming part of our lives. Yet everyone knew we were *best* friends.

Then one Saturday Eleanor came over to say she had exciting news: Her dad had bought them a new house in the St. Louis suburbs. "It's in Clayton," she said. "Wow!" I responded. Everyone knew that was where the wealthy people lived. Eleanor told me about her new school with its indoor swimming pool and her new house where she'd have her own bedroom. I hugged her and tried to sound happy. I knew I should share my best friend's joy, but inside I was scared. We'd seen each other nearly every day for the last five years, and now she'd be an hour away. That might as well have been hundreds of miles away, for parents didn't chauffeur kids then as they do today.

Eleanor was sad about leaving me, too, but she was caught up in her great adventure. That day I learned that it's much easier to be the one going away than the one who is left behind.

We vowed we'd write—every day. And for a week or two, we did. Then it became once a week, then once a month, then twice a year. We still loved each other, but we were building separate lives.

By high school we seldom talked, but I thought about her now and then and always smiled. The last letter I had from her, she was at an Ivy League college, dating the heir to a big pharmacy chain. I was planning on marrying my high school sweetheart, who wasn't rich but was full of promise.

In the years since my marriage, I've moved all over the country. And I've had three children—a lively, sweet boy and two precious girls, neither of them named Lisa. About a year ago, I found out Eleanor's married name and discovered where she was living. More years had passed than I would care to count, but I called her up anyway, just to talk. At first I felt a little nervous. But when I told her who I was, we started to giggle and squeal like schoolgirls—two middle-aged women, trading feelings and secrets just like long ago. Though the course of our lives had taken us in different directions, our treasured childhood friendship still held meaning for us both.

Eleanor was my first best friend, but I've had several more over the years. While time and distance may cause a relationship to change, a friend remains a treasure we carry in our heart. Each one brings out the best in us: "As iron sharpens iron, a friend sharpens a friend" (Prov. 27:17, NLT). Through the years I've been blessed to add new friendships along with the old ones. But some things remain the same. Best friends are always the ones with whom you share your secrets and dreams. They always think you're prettier or more talented than you really are. And they always set your heart to singing, "You belong to me, just to little ol' me."

ABCDEFGHIJKLMNOPQRSTUVWXYZ
Lo, I am with you
always, even unto
the end of the world.
Matthew 28:20
Ellen Stouffer ©1998

In Perfect Harmony

Lo, I am with you alway, even unto the end of the world.

MATTHEW 28:20, KJV

I am five years old, and my family and I are gathered on a hot summer evening under a large canvas covering for a tent meeting—a two-week-long gathering where an evangelist will preach a nightly service. We have come to this small country town at the request of some family friends. Many people have come from miles around to hear the visiting evangelist and make a "joyful noise unto the Lord"—though on this night I think God may wish he were hard of hearing. The twangy singing is about as melodious as a bagpipe and accordion duet.

The theme for the tent meeting is "Let Your Light Shine," and the theme song is "This Little Light of Mine." Although I am only a child, I know this song well because I sing it at Sunday school. The friends who have asked us to visit this meeting know I love to sing, since I can always be coaxed to perform for my parents' friends. Apparently someone has told this to the evangelist, because I hear him introducing me, and my mother urges me on stage to sing for the congregation.

Singing is as natural to me as breathing, so when the pianist plays the opening chord, I proudly sing: "This little light of mine. I'm gonna let it shine. Let it shine, let it shine, let it shine."

I am too young to appreciate that there are many forms and expressions of worship, so I am totally unprepared for what follows. People stand up and start shouting, clapping their hands, and stomping their feet. Some dance and do somersaults in the aisles. I am startled, to say the least—I never saw anyone dance at church before!

Somehow I manage to get through "Hide it under a bushel? No!" and "Don't let Satan *whuff* [blow] it out." But one time through is enough for me, and I race off the stage to the safety of my mother.

I attach myself to her leg and hide my face in her dress.

But the audience loves me. They clap and shout, "More, more!" and someone calls, "Sing it again, sister!" The evangelist coaxes me, saying, "Come on back up here, little girl."

But I'm staying safe by my mother's side. This is one little light that's going to stay hidden for a while.

I can chuckle now, remembering my fearful reaction to that service. Although it was my first experience of stage fright, it wasn't my last. When I was seven, I sang my first "special music" solo in our Sunday morning church service. The song I sang was "In the Garden." I can still recall the words: "I come to the garden alone, while the dew is still on the roses; and the voice I hear, falling on my ear, the Son of God discloses. And he walks with me, and he talks with me, and he tells me I am his own, and the joy we share, as we tarry there, none other has ever known."

Our music director, who was my voice teacher at the time, chose the song. Although I had memorized the words, I had no idea what they meant. If I truly had understood the love of God and the friendship of Jesus, I would have known that he is always with me, walking beside me—and maybe what happened to me that morning wouldn't have happened.

When I started to sing, I suddenly realized there was a sea of faces looking at me. My throat and mouth went dry. My voice cracked, and I shattered right along with it. I was so frightened at being alone in front of so many people that I couldn't sing another note.

The music director tried to help me by saying in a stage whisper, "Start over again." Though I tried, my stage fright only got worse. I uttered about two words and my voice cracked again. Suddenly I couldn't remember the words of the song. From there on, my memory of the rest of the morning is blank. I don't know if I somehow finished the song or if I sat down. I do know I was so traumatized by the experience that for many years afterward

I wouldn't sing a solo. I sang in choirs and small groups; I even sang duets and trios. But I couldn't sing alone.

There is a notation in my baby book that says, ". . . carrying a tune at age three—very unusual for a child to do this so early." I don't know if that was so unusual; more likely that observation came from a mother wanting to believe her child was exceptional. But I do know I have always had a passion for music. It has always had the power to comfort me, uplift me, and make me feel joyous. It has always been a part of the seasons of my life.

As a little child I sang, "Twinkle, twinkle, little star." Then I moved on to, "School days, good old golden rule days." At graduation I sang, "Climb every mountain 'til you find your dream," and on my wedding day, I sang, "Whither thou goest I will go."

As the spring of my life turned into summer, I sang lullabies to my babies: "Sail, baby, sail out across the sea. Only don't forget to sail home again to me." All too soon my children were leaving home to start lives on their own. I sang, "Sunrise, Sunset" and thought about how quickly the years pass.

In the winter of sadness after I'd lost my mother, I sang her favorite hymn: "Amazing grace! how sweet the sound—that saved a wretch like me! I once was lost but now am found, was blind but now I see."

As I think about these sweet melodies, I realize that music is a metaphor for life—there are highs and lows, sharps and flats, discords and harmonies. But the most melodious times in my life are those times when I am in perfect harmony with my God. From the corridors of memory I hear my childish voice singing "In the Garden"—but now the words are meaningful to me: "He speaks, and the sound of his voice is so sweet the birds hush their singing, and the melody that he brings to me within my heart is ringing. And he walks with me, and he talks with me, and he tells me I am his own, and the joy we share as we tarry there, none other has ever known."

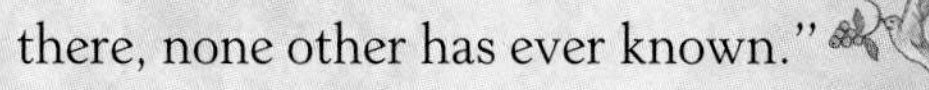

ABCDEFGHIJKLMNOPQRSTUVWXYZ
BOATS
Allen Stouffer © 1986
Oct 1986
Let your light shine before men in such a way that they may see your good works, and glorify your Father who is in heaven. Matthew 5:16

Lighthouse Summer

Let your light shine before men in such a way that they may see your good works, and glorify your Father who is in heaven.

MATTHEW 5:16, NASB

As a young child, I loved to press a conch shell to my ear, close my eyes, and listen to what sounded like the roar of the sea—dreaming that someday I might travel to see the ocean. When I was ten years old my dream came true. Our neighbor, Mrs. Riley, offered to take me with her to spend a month at her daughter's summerhouse at the New Jersey shore. Her daughter had just had twins, and she wanted her mother to come help her with the babies and her older son, Robby.

Robby was my age, and we often played together when he came to visit his grandmother. He was a regular "Dennis the Menace." For example, two summers before, Robby had decided to jump off the roof of his grandmother's garage, convinced he could fly. No amount of arguing from me could persuade him otherwise, and while I was running to warn his grandmother, Robby had taken flight. Fortunately, in light of how dangerous this stunt was, the worst damage Robby had sustained was a broken arm.

After Robby's rooftop experience, Mrs. Riley had instructed me to tell her right away if he suggested any other perilous feats of daring. That's probably why she made her generous offer to take me with her to the New Jersey shore. Mrs. Riley told my mother she thought a playmate for Robby would help keep him occupied—and, I thought, out of trouble.

Our trip began with a long Greyhound bus ride to New York, where Robby and his family met us. From there, Mr. Murphy, Robby's dad, drove us to the shore. As the seaside drew near, the air began to smell of salt and fish. Then we rounded a curve and the vast ocean stretched before us. I caught a glimpse of a tall red-and-white lighthouse.

"Look! There's the lighthouse," I said excitedly. Mr. Murphy had already told me about Barnegat lighthouse and promised he'd take us for a visit the following day.

"I've climbed all the way up to the top," Robby bragged.

I wondered about the wisdom of that, remembering Robby's

penchant for leaps from tall structures.

The next day Mr. Murphy took Robby and me to tour the lighthouse. It was a beautiful day—sunlight glistened on the water, and off in the distance sailboats bobbed up and down like tiny toys against the horizon. The setting was so peaceful that I was surprised when the lighthouse guide said the waters were dangerous to navigate because of the northeast winds. Before the lighthouse had been built, many shipwrecks had occurred along the coast.

"Were any of them pirate ships, and is there buried treasure?" Robby asked.

"Hush, Robby," his dad said. "Just be still and listen."

I could see Robby's mischievous smile, and I imagined the next misdeed would involve diving for treasure.

We learned that the first light station had a light so weak it was often impossible to tell if it was a ship's light or a lighthouse. The guide told us that the present-day Barnegat lighthouse was built in 1855. It was 150 feet tall and built on a rise 30 feet above the ocean. With the new lighthouse's greater height and stronger beacon, its light could be seen far out at sea.

"Does the light still work?" Robby wanted to know.

"It's not in use anymore," the guide told him. "The lighthouse was retired in 1944 when its job was taken over by a lightship anchored offshore."

By then Robby was bouncing around, so his dad suggested we climb to the top of the tower. Once up there, Robby was full of questions about what this wheel did and what that knob was for, but I just wanted to take in the view. As far as I could see there were miles and miles of ocean. I wondered how far one would have to travel to reach the other shore, and I thought about what an adventure it must be to sail across the ocean. It both awed and frightened me, but I had no idea how soon we would experience our own peril on the sea.

The next day was especially hot, and Mr. Murphy suggested we take the boat and go fishing. Robby thought it was a great idea, but I was a little afraid to go out on the water in a small boat.

"Girls are just scaredy-cats," Robby taunted.

So of course I had to go. Donning life jackets, we headed out into the ocean. I was just starting to relax when Robby said he wanted to get into the water to cool off. His dad said he could go, but knowing Robby's tendency for getting into trouble, Mr. Murphy insisted on tying one end of a rope to Robby's life vest and the other end to the boat. He said that would keep Robby from getting too far away.

As soon as Robby was in the water he started diving, doing funny tricks, and showing off. Then a sudden breeze came up, which sent the boat swinging on its anchor. Next thing we knew, Robby was choking. Thinking he was being funny, he had wrapped the rope around his neck several times. Now the current was pulling him one way and the boat was swaying the other. We

couldn't get enough slack to loosen the rope.

Robby's dad was frantic, and I was nearly paralyzed with fear. All I could think to do was pray. Then I heard someone yelling, "Here's a knife!" I opened my eyes in time to see a boat pull alongside us and a man toss a pocketknife to Robby's dad. Mr. Murphy caught the knife, opened the blade, and with one quick thrust sliced the rope in two. There were quick cheers all around.

Once Robby was back on board and we knew he was okay, the men began discussing the event. The man with the knife said he'd felt compelled to sharpen his knife that morning—and because of this it was sharp enough to cut the rope in one quick swipe. He said he didn't always carry his pocketknife, but after sharpening it he'd just dropped it in his pocket. And the fact that he had been close enough to see the commotion was also a miracle. Everyone marveled at the amazing "coincidences," but I was certain Robby's rescue was an answer to my prayer. Now that I'm grown, I can think of many such times in my life when God has provided the way out of a disaster long before I even knew there was a problem.

I don't know if Robby learned anything that summer, but I started to see many things in new ways. I had memorized a verse in Sunday school where Jesus said, "I am the light of the world: he that followeth me shall not walk in darkness, but shall have the light of life" (John 8:12, KJV). After visiting the lighthouse and hearing all the stories about the ships saved from disaster by having its light to follow, I more clearly understood the metaphor of that verse. I also realized that when we belong to Jesus, his light shines within us—and we, too, can become a light in the darkness.

I have many sweet memories of that month at the shore—bonfires on the beach and toasted marshmallows, building sand castles and collecting shells, the friendship of Robby and his family—but I never think of it without remembering the lighthouse and the rescue provided for us by the Light of the World.

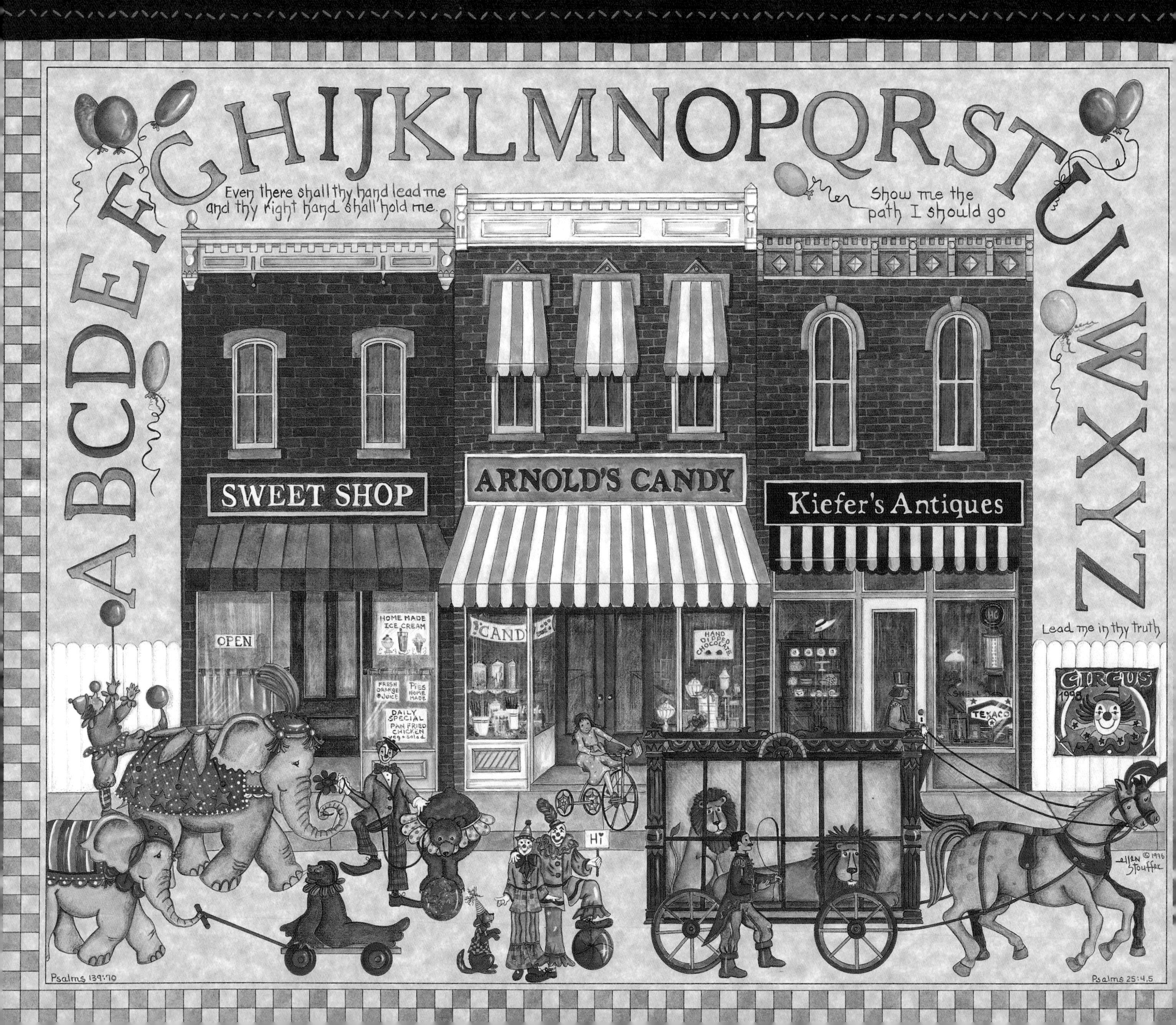
ABCDEFGHIJKLMNOPQRSTUVWXYZ
Even there shall thy hand lead me
and thy right hand shall hold me.
Show me the
path I should go
Lead me in thy truth
SWEET SHOP
ARNOLD'S CANDY
Kiefer's Antiques
OPEN
HOME MADE
ICE CREAM
FRESH
ORANGE
JUICE
PIES
HOME
MADE
DAILY
SPECIAL
PAN FRIED
CHICKEN
veg + salad
CANDY
HAND
DIPPED
CHOCOLATE
TEXACO
CIRCUS
HI
ellen Stouffer © 1996
Psalms 139:70
Psalms 25:4,5

The Greatest Show On Earth

Even there shall thy hand lead me, and thy right hand shall hold me.

PSALM 139:10, KJV

"Ladies and gentlemen, children of all ages, step right up and meet the most astonishing assemblage of remarkable performers The Greatest Show On Earth has ever known!"

It was the summer I was eight years old, and the Ringling Bros. and Barnum & Bailey Circus had come to town with its big tents, menagerie of animals, and spectacular acts. I had been anxiously awaiting the trip to St. Louis to see it, and finally the evening had arrived. As the lights dimmed and the spotlight shined on the ringmaster, he uttered the famous welcome that still opens the circus today.

The drums rolled and a bevy of colored lights flashed back and forth over the various rings where the entertainers would soon perform. Then the parade began—performers in glittering costumes marched in a long procession, waving to the cheering crowd. There were trapeze artists, acrobats, tightrope walkers, and clowns. Animal acts abounded—barking sea lions, prancing horses, dancing bears, and lumbering elephants—all making a colorful and exciting entrance in their spangled decorations and tasseled, feathered caps.

Once the last of the cavalcade made its way across the center ring, the ringmaster said, "And now, without further ado, I'd like to direct your attention to . . ." There were more drum rolls, and the spotlight swung to the ringmaster's right as he announced, ". . . the most death-defying act the world has ever seen: Marvin the Magnificent!" The music began as a tightrope walker pranced high above our heads, without the benefit of a safety net below. A collective *"aaaahhh"* rose from the crowd, and we held our breath when he appeared to totter and almost fall—one leg outstretched for balance, his long pole bobbing up and down. But he soon regained his footing and we could breathe again.

We were held spellbound by acts each seemingly more spectacular than the one before. It was especially frightening to see lions and tigers leap through burning hoops and walk on barrels only a few feet from where we sat. Just when I thought I couldn't stand the tension any longer, funny clowns rode in on bicycles to frolic and make us laugh.

Every act was announced in a superlative and

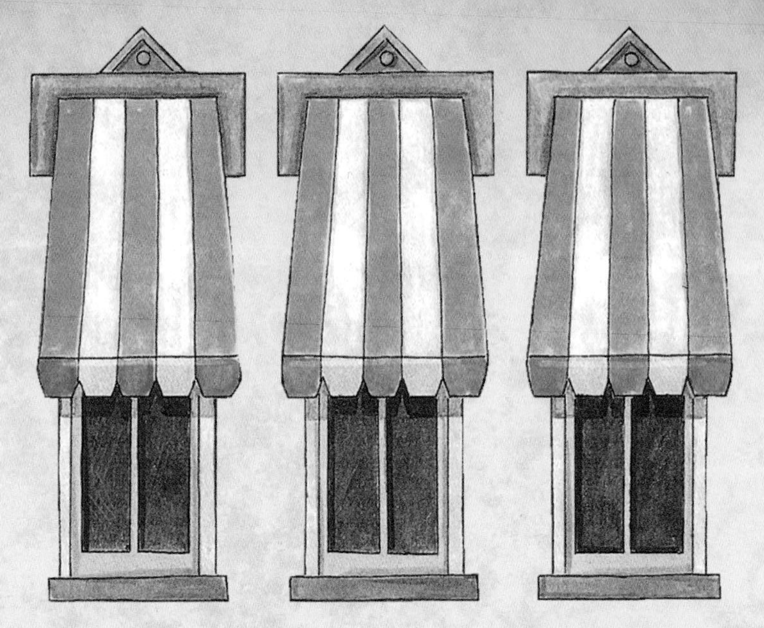

grandiose way. An elephant wasn't just an elephant, it was "The Most Towering Monarch of His Mighty Race." Performers "astonished," "dazzled," and "defied death." Since this was the first circus I'd ever attended, I had no idea that this boasting was in the great tradition of the circus's founder, P. T. Barnum. He was known around the world as "Master Showman" and "Patron Saint of Promoters." Perhaps even more to the point, he was said to have given the nineteenth-century public "shameless hucksterism, peerless spectacle, and everything in between."

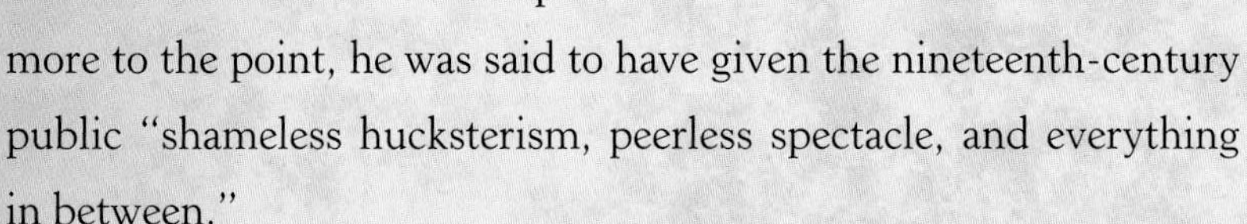

While it may not be true, Barnum is said to have coined the phrase, "There's a sucker born every minute." Whether he was just a great promoter or a master deceiver, the gullible public flocked to see Barnum's wonders. One infamous story about him took place in 1841 at Scudder's American Museum in New York. People were said to come from every corner of the globe to see his spectacular exhibit of more than "500,000 natural and artificial curiosities." One of the signs he posted in the museum announced: "This way to the egress." Not knowing that "egress" was another word for exit, people followed the sign and then had to pay another quarter to reenter the museum.

But if Barnum sometimes took advantage of the crowd, they seemed to delight in being bilked, for thousands thronged to see the oddities he promoted in his Grand Traveling Museum, Menagerie, Caravan, and Circus. He exhibited everything from "The Feejee Mermaid," supposedly an embalmed mermaid purchased near Calcutta, to a 161-year-old woman who claimed to have been the nurse of George Washington. A consummate showman, Barnum coined the term, "The Greatest Show On Earth" to describe his circus—and people agreed it was.

Today, when cinematography with computerized special effects is commonplace, a circus seems tame. But from the late 1800s up until the advent of a television set in every home, the circus offered drama, suspense, and wonder. Although there was a good deal of puffery and occasionally even a con, people seemed only too willing to pay their money for an opportunity to be amazed.

Like most people, I'd like to think I'm far too sophisticated to be taken in by the claims presented in Barnum's early shows. But the truth is, far too often I'm one of those suckers. I fall for the ploys that Satan, the great deceiver, presents. In his own way a great showman and promoter, he makes wrongdoings seem "dazzling" and "astonishing" too.

God has warned me of Satan's treachery: "Take heed lest your heart be deceived, and you turn aside and serve other gods and worship them" (Deut. 11:16, RSV).

Yet sometimes, even with the best intentions, it's difficult for me to discern what's truth and what's a lie. I feel a bit like Marvin the Magnificent trying to balance myself on a slender thread—concerned that a wrong move might send me careening out of control. But God's Word steadies me. Unlike Marvin, I have the benefit of a safety net—the strong, comforting, outstretched arms of God.

It's a beautiful world that God has made—truly a "peerless spectacle." Yet as we travel through life, we will also sometimes have to face "shameless hucksterism . . . and everything in between." For those who trust and follow the Lord, however, the greatest show is not one here on earth, but the one we look forward to in heaven.

Blessed is he whose hope is in the Lord... Who made heaven and earth, the sea and all that is in them; Who keeps faith forever. Psalms 146:5,6

Sisters

Blessed is he . . . whose hope is in the Lord . . . Who made heaven and earth, the sea and all that is in them; Who keeps faith forever.

PSALM 146:5-6, NASB

In my mother's photo box, there were many faded black-and-white photographs of my older sister, Judy, and me taken with my dad's old box-style Kodak Brownie camera. In one we stand bundled like a pair of Eskimos, waiting our turn to see a Woolworth Santa. In another we are dressed in our Easter finery, complete with shiny new Mary Janes, white cotton gloves, and spring bonnets. A year later we are squinting into the sunshine as we sit having a summer picnic. Though the settings are different, one thing remains the same: we are always connected—her arm around my shoulders or her hand holding mine. The gesture is symbolic of our relationship, which goes deeper than friendship: we are *sisters.*

According to our mother, we began forging a bond from the day Judy first saw me. Mother said her eyes grew round as saucers and she begged to hold me. She's held me in one way or another ever since—coaching me through my first day of school, my first date, and my first love. She's nursed me through skinned knees and broken hearts. Our "sisterhood" has endured—although miles have separated us geographically, we remain close in our hearts.

Judy always seemed special to me. Since I'm almost six years younger, she knew how to do everything better than I did. From tying shoes to manipulating buttons into tiny buttonholes, my hands were all thumbs—hers all quick and nimble fingers. Much of what I know today, she taught me.

My adoration for her was so strong that even when she wasn't with me, I was thinking about her. If the nurse at the doctor's office gave me a sucker, I would tell her, "I have a sister." She'd laugh and give me another so I could take it home to share with Judy. We always shared everything—our bedroom, our secrets, our dreams.

I remember many nights lying in the big double bed we shared, with the room dark and quiet except for the occasional creak and moan that houses seem to acquire as they age and settle. I was certain the sound came from something alive.

"Judy," I whispered to her in the darkness, "I'm scared. There's something under the bed."

"There's nothing under the bed, silly," she said. "Come here."

I'd roll over closer and she'd wrap her arms around me. "How about a story?" she'd ask. Soon I'd fall asleep as she spun a fanciful tale she'd made up about a little girl—just like me.

Although I had many playmates of my own, I was happiest when

I was allowed to tag along with my sister. Most of the time I don't think Judy minded having me as her shadow, although now and then I'm sure I was a bother. Like the time we went on a church trip to the St. Louis Zoo. I was seven; Judy was almost thirteen. She and her friends had commandeered the back of the church bus—the long seat that could easily hold six giggly preteen girls.

At the start of the trip, I resigned myself to the fate of staying with the other six- and seven-year-olds at the front of the bus. However, by the end of the day, I wanted to be with my sister. After we had boarded the bus to go home, some of the children in my group decided they needed to use the bathroom. Our chaperone rounded up the ones who wanted to go and rushed them off the bus.

I seized this opportunity to walk back and initiate myself into my sister's group. They seemed to be having a grand time—eating popcorn and sharing jokes. I asked Judy if I could sit with her. When she brushed me aside, I said I needed to go to the bathroom and my leader was gone. She'd have to take me. With a big sigh, she excused herself from her friends and shuffled me off the bus.

The St. Louis Zoo is a big place, but Judy recalled a restroom in the concession stand. Holding my hand, she hurried me back to the place she remembered. When we arrived there was a long line, but Judy waited patiently until it was my turn. Then she led me back to the parking lot. A sea of yellow-and-white buses waited, belching out their acrid fumes. However, our bus was nowhere in sight. We marched up and down the rows, with Judy scrutinizing names and numbers, until she confirmed her worst fear—the bus had left without us.

"Don't worry. I'm sure they'll be back soon to get us," she assured me.

Time passed and there was still no sign of the bus. As the blue summer sky turned to evening gray, Judy announced we should return to the concession stand, where she was certain there'd be a pay phone. "I'll just call Daddy," she said, knowing he'd find a solution even though he was more than an hour away.

Arriving at the concession stand, we discovered that the wooden shutters had been pulled over the window and all the doors were locked up for the night. The look of dismay on my sister's face made me start to cry.

"Don't cry. I'll take care of you," she said. "Don't I always? I think we just need to say a little prayer. Remember what you learned in Sunday school? The Bible says, 'He orders his angels to protect you wherever you go' (Ps. 91:11, NLT). We'll just ask God to send an angel to watch over us."

Obediently, I bowed my head as Judy uttered a prayer for our safety. We had just lifted our heads when we saw a chubby, gray-haired security guard hurrying our way. "If you get lost, find a policeman," our parents always told us. The guard in his gray uniform and silver badge looked enough like a policeman to instill confidence in us, so Judy explained our predicament. After hearing our story, the guard assured us he would stay with us until the bus returned. He seemed a peculiar kind of angel, but I was sure God had sent him just the same.

When the bus returned, we learned that they had been halfway home before one of my sister's friends began to wonder why Judy had stayed up front with me rather than coming back with them. It was only when she went to look that she discovered we were missing and spread the alarm.

The "incident at the zoo," as it came to be called, had been a risky situation—two little girls alone in a big city park at dusk. Yet just as my sister promised, she'd taken care of me—something she continues to do to this day. When a few years ago our mother lay dying, I sat holding her hand and weeping, while Judy stood patting my shoulder and comforting me. Too weak to talk, Mother looked up only once to smile and nod, as if reassuring herself that Judy and I would continue to share the caring bond of "sisterhood."

Almost forty years have passed since we shared a room, but in Judy's mind I'm still the "baby." Not long ago we got together for a family celebration. We were working together in the kitchen when she handed me a casserole to warm up in the oven. "Don't forget to take the plastic wrap off first," she cautioned me. I just rolled my eyes in response, and we broke into peals of laughter thinking about the absurd thing she'd said. But old habits die hard—and who can blame her for instructing me? She still remembers me when I was all thumbs.

ABCDEFGHIJKLMNOPQRSTUVWXYZ
My cup runneth over
Psalm 23:5
goodness and lovingkindness will
follow me all the days of my life,
Psalm 23:6
AUCTION
Today
SOAP
GERANIUMS

Give Thanks

My cup runneth over. Surely goodness and mercy shall follow me all the days of my life.

PSALM 23:5-6, KJV

Thanksgiving was only a couple of weeks away. Since we would be spending it with Mother's family, we were having an early celebration with Daddy's relatives in the Ozarks.

"I'm grateful we have a sunny day to travel," Daddy commented as we wound our way west, leaving St. Louis behind.

But all I was feeling was cranky. I asked again for the fourth time in an hour, "How much farther is it?"

"We're barely on our way," Daddy answered. "Honey, why don't you relax and enjoy the drive. Look how pretty everything is."

Then he started to point out the beauty along the way—the trees with their crimson and yellow leaves sparkling in the sun against the blue horizon. A small waterfall that trickled over the rocks, forming a little stream below. "The Lord sure gave us a wonderful world," he said.

It was just like Daddy to be thankful. He frequently reminded my sister and me of the Bible verse, "In every thing give thanks" (1 Thess. 5:18, KJV).

"Look at that," he said again, calling my attention to a hawk that swooped and soared over the mountaintop. "Just listen." And we heard the large bird keening—*scree, scree.*

"Isn't he majestic?" Daddy asked me.

A few minutes later, he pointed out a pair of groundhogs scuttling into the woods. "You'd better keep your eyes open or you might miss something," he warned me.

Soon Daddy was keeping me entertained with stories about his boyhood—about catching frogs in the pond or picking wild blackberries for cobblers. He called my attention to a weathered red barn topped with a whirligig, a tall round silo filled with grain, and an old abandoned country store. This prompted a story about the general store in the town where he grew up—the town's social center. Everything that happened in his small town was passed around as the old men sat playing checkers and whittling.

"If we took a watermelon from a farmer's field, our dad would know it by the time we got home for supper! Made you real careful about what you did," Daddy joked.

When we spotted an old barn with household goods out front, Mother said, "Look, honey, an auction!" Daddy was already slowing down, knowing she'd love to stop and browse. Although my mother didn't collect antiques, she loved beautiful needlework and was out of the car in a flash, heading toward a stack of colorful quilts.

Before long, I noticed Mother and Daddy conversing with a woman who was sitting and watching the auction. As they talked, Daddy discovered she knew some of his cousins who lived in a neighboring town. Soon they were chatting like old friends.

The woman—whose name, we learned, was Eva Hanson—invited us to come up on the porch for donuts and a glass of apple cider. As she and my parents talked, I learned that Mrs. Hanson had been widowed three years before. She had tried to keep the farm going with the help of some farmhands. However, three years of near drought had yielded few crops and little income, so the bank had foreclosed on her farm.

"I've lived here for over fifty years," she told us. "I came here as a bride."

I wasn't sure what "foreclose" was, but from Mother and Daddy's looks of concern and words of sympathy, I knew it was something bad. Mrs. Hanson didn't complain, though. Instead she shared stories of their happy years on the farm, the joys of their family life, and how fortunate she was to have raised five wonderful children. She was going to live with her daughter in Ohio.

"Now that's a real blessing," she told us. "Just think, I'll be able to see my grandchildren grow up instead of seeing them only once or twice a year."

Throughout Mrs. Hanson's conversation, she praised God for his goodness, even though tears occasionally came to her eyes.

"It's a hard thing having to leave this old place behind," she told us. "But God will go with me, and I believe he must have some wonderful things just waiting for me. 'In every thing give thanks,' " she quoted.

Mother and Daddy smiled and nodded their understanding.

After a while, Daddy said we had to get on our way, and we wished her well. When we arrived at the car, Mother and Daddy had a whispered conversation and Daddy returned to the auction. He returned a short time later, smiling brightly and carrying an apple pie.

"From Mrs. Hanson," Daddy explained to Mother. "She insisted I take it."

"Did you get the quilt?" Mother asked expectantly.

Daddy nodded.

"What quilt?" I asked. I didn't see anything in Daddy's hands other than the apple pie.

"Oh, there was a quilt I wanted Daddy to buy," Mother said.

"Where is it?" I persisted.

"He gave it to Mrs. Hanson," Mother said.

"But wasn't it her quilt to begin with?" I asked.

Mother patiently explained that Mrs. Hanson had to sell all her things to settle the debt on the farm. When Mother had complimented her on a beautiful wedding-ring quilt, she learned Mrs. Hanson's mother had made it and given it to her on her wedding day. Mother had Daddy buy the quilt and return it to Mrs. Hanson.

"At first she seemed reluctant to take it back, but when I told her it would make us happy, she cried tears of joy," Daddy said. "I think giving us the pie helped her express her gratitude and preserve her self-esteem. So I just asked her how she knew apple pie was my favorite!"

As we continued our drive, Mother suggested we play a Thanksgiving game. She asked my sister and me each to make a list of all the things for which we were grateful. When we returned home from our trip, she said, we'd cut paper leaves from construction paper and transfer the items from our list onto them. Then she'd have Daddy cut a small tree branch, and we could hang our leaves on it. At Thanksgiving dinner, we would read the leaves from our "blessing tree." I thought this was a great idea and stayed busy making my list. As I wrote, I thought about Mrs. Hanson, who had lost everything but was still thanking God for the blessings of her life.

Now when Thanksgiving draws near, I often remember that day at Mrs. Hanson's farm. What a tragic event—to lose her husband and then her home and all her possessions. Yet despite this, she kept her faith in God and continued to thank him in all things.

The lessons I learned that day still linger in my heart. I learned that joy is not found in material possessions. Life's real blessings are found in the beauty of God's creation, the joy of home and family, and the miracle of God's never-ending love for us. I'm glad my parents taught me not only to notice my blessings, but also to express my gratitude for them. There is an old saying: "An ungrateful man is like a hog under a tree eating apples and never looking up to see where they come from."

I wonder if that was what Daddy was thinking about when he told me, "Keep your eyes open or you might miss something." 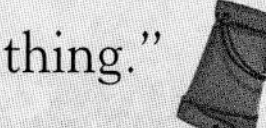

FRIENDS LOVE AT ALL TIMES
DAIRY
Bonnie's Raspberry Jelly
APPLE BUTTER
To a special friend
BUTTER

Preserving Friendship

A friend loves at all times.

PROVERBS 17:17, NASB

Outside my window, the snow is falling in giant flakes. The house next door is mantled in white, and with its snow-covered pines it looks like a Christmas card. It's early morning, and most of the neighborhood is still sleeping.

Inside my cozy kitchen I feel safe, warm, and content. The wonderful aroma of cinnamon rolls permeates the room—and is partly responsible for this feeling that "all's right with the world." For me, the smell of cinnamon evokes memories that are synonymous with love—my grandma's and mother's warm, welcoming kitchens, filled with the smells of Christmas cookies or cinnamon crisp baking in the oven and spiced apples or apple butter simmering on the stove.

I come from a long line of good cooks, and the kitchen has always been the heart of our homes—where we congregate to talk, laugh, and share the events of our day. When I was a child I especially liked the days when my mother, her sisters, and Grandma would get together to "put up" fruits, vegetables, jelly, jam, or apple butter—my favorite. Canning was such a big task that it was often done in tandem with relatives and friends. The camaraderie and many helping hands made the day's work more fun.

Even after Grandma was up in years, she would often lend a hand, offer guidance, or oversee the work in the busy kitchen. I can still see her wearing her sensible bib-type apron and practical orthopedic shoes, with her white hair pulled into a taut bun. Her round face would alternate between delighted smiles and arched eyebrows, depending on whether her daughters' conversation pleased or annoyed her—the latter usually occurring when they disregarded her advice. My mother and her sisters were all women with strong opinions—a trait more admired than disapproved of in our family. I believe that secretly Grandma was pleased she hadn't raised mousy daughters, for most of the time they all got along happily. Canning day was filled with laughter and shared confidences.

When Grandma was a girl, it was essential to preserve the harvest. Much of the food was homegrown, and it was necessary to make it

last throughout the winter. After harvest, many days were spent putting up fruits and vegetables in Mason jars. These were then taken to a root cellar or another cool place, where they were lined up on rows of shelves—a tangible sign that the family would have enough food until the next growing season.

Canning was an art handed down from mother to daughter. We had lots of family recipes for everything from Grandma's bread-and-butter pickles to her spiced fruit. But the recipe we treasured most was for Grandma's apple butter.

Grandma said that when she was a girl, apple butter was made outdoors, using huge copper kettles over an open fire. It was always a family event, with many relatives gathering to peel the apples and stew them slowly in the big pot. Someone had to stand nearby and stir the ingredients frequently with a long wooden paddle. The process usually took the entire day.

At our house, however, apple butter was made in large pots on the stove. But the rest of the procedure and the recipe was much the same as in Grandma's childhood. The process still took many hours, as bushels of apples were peeled and then slowly stewed in apple cider. When the time was deemed "just right"—a point usually determined by Grandma—sugar, cinnamon, cloves, and the rest of the ingredients for the "secret" recipe were added. But the hours of work were well worth the effort. Even on a cold winter day, a jar of Grandma's apple butter could be hauled up from the basement and slathered onto hot buttered biscuits. My mouth still waters at the thought.

After Grandma passed away, the last jars of her apple butter were shared among her six daughters. I don't know about my aunts, but my mother carefully rationed the jars, and we slowly savored their contents. It was a sad day when mother announced we were

opening the last jar of Grandma's apple butter. My mother, whom I thought was the world's best cook, said no one made apple butter that tasted as good as her mother's. Even though she used her mother's recipe, Mother declared that hers never tasted the same. Having experienced the same phenomenon with my mother's special recipes, I've concluded they lack a crucial ingredient—the loving hand that made them.

Although we still cherish the old family recipes, canning has become a lost art with my generation and my children's. But the legacy of love and friendship, passed on from mother to daughter, sister to sister, and friend to friend, is still nourished and kindled in our kitchens. It's there that we talk, laugh, and share some of our best secrets. Even though we don't make apple butter anymore, we still preserve a secret family recipe—friendship.

TOYS
94
Thanks be unto God for His unspeakable Gift
2 Cor. 9:15
RRY
CHRISTMAS
ellen stouffer ©1992

The Gift

Thanks be unto God for his unspeakable gift.
2 CORINTHIANS 9:15, KJV

Christmas, 1952—The house is silent except for the occasional popping of a floorboard and the *whoosh* of air as the furnace blower kicks on. But even the slightest sound sends me scurrying to the window to draw back the curtain and see if it's morning yet. Finally the blackness of night seems to have paled to a dusky gray. Surely the sun will peep over the horizon soon, I think anxiously.

My sister, Judy, is tossing and turning too. "Is it morning yet?" she whispers.

A fresh snowfall covers the ground. Most houses up and down our block are still dark, but here and there I see a light in a window and the twinkle of outdoor Christmas lights. Then I see it—the pale pinkish tint that signals the rising of the sun. "It's here!" I whisper back, wanting to shout. "It's Christmas!"

Judy rushes to the window, and together we bask in the anticipation and joy of Christmas morning. We hug one another and whisper and giggle, knowing we aren't supposed to wake up our parents too early. But secretly I hope we are making enough noise that they'll hear us and get up.

This is always the hardest part of Christmas morning—the waiting. It's a rule at our house that we can't go downstairs to see what Santa has brought until Daddy gets up and turns on the lights of the Christmas tree, which give the room a magical glow. Tradition dictates that when he is ready with the camera and the lights to capture our first glimpse of the tree, Mother will call up the stairs, "Merry Christmas!"—our signal that it's okay to go downstairs.

Finally we hear our parents stirring. "Put on your robe and slippers," Judy orders, and I quickly obey. We both want to be ready to go when we get the call. I hear the creak of the stairway door, and Mother's cheery voice calls, "Are you up yet?" We laugh, knowing she's heard us rustling and giggly for what seems like hours. "Merry Christmas!" she announces as we jostle for position and rush down the stairs.

All the lights are off except for the twinkling lights of the tree, reflected in the shimmering strands of tinsel. There beneath the tree is the most beautiful ballerina doll I have ever seen. She's blonde and blue-eyed and has on a sparkling blue tutu and pale-pink ballet slippers. She's more wonderful than anything I imagined, and I rush to pick her up.

Judy picks up a large package wrapped in shiny red paper with a big silver bow. I hug my doll and watch her delight as she opens the box to discover a beautiful red velvet coat trimmed with a white fur collar.

We take turns opening our gifts, savoring the excitement as each of us tears off the bright wrappings to reveal the next treasure. For Judy, there's the camera she's been dreaming about, an angora sweater, and a plaid pleated skirt made by Mother. For me, there's a doll's suitcase filled with a wardrobe for my new ballerina doll. For weeks the sewing room door has been closed, and I know the outfits have been handmade by Mother, whom I understand is sometimes Santa's helper. I marvel at how beautiful the doll clothes are. Both Judy and I have new books and a game. Mother has also sewn a special Christmas dress for each of us. And there's an unexpected surprise for me—a dollhouse filled with miniature furniture. I don't know it, but these have been designed and built for me by Daddy in his basement workshop. The morning sparkles all around us, shimmering like the star that graces the top of our tree.

Later today we will dress in our new Christmas outfits, gather up more gifts of love—along with Mother's famous coconut cream pies—and head for a huge family dinner at Aunt Tillie's house. Grandma and Grandpa will be there, along with Mother's other sisters and their husbands and children. But for now, it's just the four of us—secure and happy in our time together.

Mother's face beams with joy. I can see she's pleased by the happiness all her hard work has brought us. Daddy looks content too, relaxing with his coffee. We don't realize he's been up half the night assembling and finishing my dollhouse. In fact, neither Judy nor I understands the work, time, and love that have gone into giving us this elaborate Christmas celebration. We will be grown and caught up in our own tradition of making Christmas special for our children before we truly understand our parents' sacrificial giving.

But then, sacrificial giving is what Christmas is all about: "For God so loved the world that he gave his only Son, so that everyone who believes in him will not perish but have eternal life" (John 3:16, NLT). What makes Christmas shimmer and sparkle—a day like no other day—is the miracle of that most incredible gift.

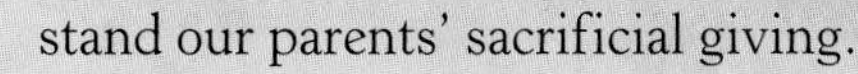

Peace on Earth
Goodwill to all men
Luke 2:14
ellen Stouffer
© 1996

The Beggar and the Star

Glory to God in the highest, and on earth peace, good will toward men.

LUKE 2:14, KJV

I have gone there often in memory—the room shimmering in the glow of flickering candles and twinkling Christmas-tree lights, hushed and still. My mother sits in the center of a circle of women, members of her Sunday school class who have gathered at our house this evening for their annual Christmas party. With her sweet smile and strawberry-blond curls, Mother looks like an angel to me. Even as young as I am, I understand there is a power in her presence as she speaks. Her voice starts off softly as she begins to recite an old poem, "The Beggar and the Star," by Vivian Laramore Rader.

There came to my door a beggar,
In the dim December light,
To ask for a crust and a corner
Where he might stay for the night.
My house was already crowded,
My food, a meager store;
So I said, "I'm very sorry,
But you'll have to ask next door."

Mother's voice rises and falls dramatically. She grew up memorizing poems, and her recitations are an expected and loved part of our family life. I've inherited her passion for beautiful words and spellbinding imagery. As I listen to the poem, I can't imagine my mother turning away anyone who was needy. "It's more blessed to give than to receive," she often reminds my sister and me.

Mother believes deeply in the giving spirit of Christmas. One has only to look around the room to see she has taken great care to make everything perfect for her guests tonight. For weeks she has polished and cleaned, cooked and baked, and spent many hours preparing little gifts for each guest. They will dine on fine china, eat with gleaming silver, and drink from crystal goblets. We are not a wealthy family, but my mother extends the best she has to visitors.

My thoughts return to the poem, as the narrator continues talking to the beggar at her door:

" . . . I can bring you tea I've
been saving
For a very special guest."
He looked at me for a moment, . . .
"Not dressed as I am dressed?"
"Oh, no," I said, "to be honest,
I've never liked beggars much,
They've always seemed unworthy,
Unclean in thought and touch."

> "And so we come again to Christmas with all its color and joy, its magic and wonder, its spirit of goodwill and warmth. But how do we come to Christmas? What it means to us depends on what we bring to it, not in gifts and outer display, but in the inner offerings of love and faith that abide in the heart"
>
> Juita Carmack

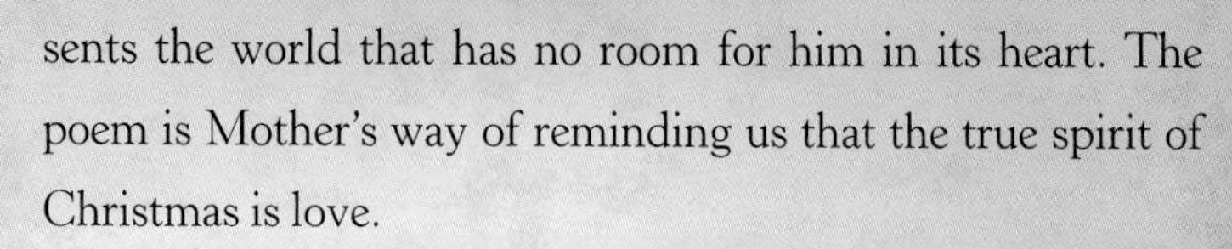

The words remind me of the Sunday we went to St. Louis and met a beggar on the street. He was asking for coins and said he was hungry. Instead of giving him money, my father invited him into the restaurant where we were going and told him he would pay for his meal. As we entered the restaurant in our church finery, accompanied by a dirty, ragged beggar, some people looked at us curiously. Others eyed us with contempt. But my dad treated the beggar with politeness and respect, and Daddy's demeanor conveyed to the restaurant staff that they were to do the same. The beggar declined to sit with us, choosing instead a back corner table where he consumed huge amounts of food. When he had eaten, he nodded quickly to my dad as he started to leave. But Daddy walked over and extended his hand to the man. The beggar took it with his right hand and covered it in a warm clasp with his left. Then he seemed to grow taller, straightening his back, as he walked from the restaurant with great dignity.

And I saw that his rags were glowing
Like garments of finest gold,
And his face was young as tomorrow,
Though I knew that the man was old . . .
And I thought of the homeless thousands
Who trudge the world today,
And I said, "Forgive me, Master,
I'm begging you to stay."

By the time Mother reaches this point in the poem, it is obvious to the women from her Sunday school class, and to me, that this poem is an allegory—the beggar represents Christ, and the narrator represents the world that has no room for him in its heart. The poem is Mother's way of reminding us that the true spirit of Christmas is love.

That poem moved me deeply as a child, but it wasn't until I was an adult that the message of the poem came to life for me. In addition to managing a home and raising three young children, I had recently returned to work. That year the thought of the approaching holidays filled me with dread instead of my usual joy. All I could think of were the extras the season seemed to call for—spending money, shopping, baking, writing cards, and decorating. I couldn't see how I was going to get everything done in time—it felt as if the only verse of the Christmas story I could relate to was, "And they came with haste. . . ." I neither noticed nor thought about the "homeless thousands." I resented the bell ringers on street corners and the charitable requests that crowded my mailbox—they only added to the pressure I already felt.

Three days before Christmas, Mother called to ask for my help. She'd just heard of a family who'd lost everything they had in a house fire. The household included a father and two little girls. According to the information Mother had, the mother of this family had died earlier that year from cancer.

Mother said she could buy the groceries, but she wondered if I would shop for the little girls. I was so far behind with my own shopping and preparation that I really wanted to say I was much too busy, but I just couldn't say no to her. Then she asked if I would help her wrap and deliver these gifts the morning of Christmas Eve. Grudgingly, I agreed.

When we arrived at the family's apartment that morning, it was small and dreary, and the father seemed listless and sad. There was no sign of the holiday—not even a tiny tree. One of the children was just a baby, and the other little girl, whose name was Alice, was five. As soon as I saw her, I regretted my hasty shopping. She welcomed us with a sweet smile, and her eyes were wide with excitement as she noticed the gift-wrapped presents along with the basket of food.

"Did you bring something for my sister?" she asked me.

"Yes," I told her. "And something for you, too."

"What about for my daddy?" she whispered. "Mommy always took me to buy a present for him. But she's up in heaven now with the angels."

I was embarrassed, as I'd only bought gifts for the chidren. "I'm sorry, sweetheart," I said. "I don't have a present for your daddy other than the basket of food."

She considered that for a moment and then asked, "Do you think maybe you could take back my gift and get something for Daddy? He's been awfully sad with Mommy gone, and I'd like to see him smile."

It was all I could do to keep my tears from falling as I promised I'd be back with a gift for her dad. Mother didn't even question me when I asked if she had time to go with me to the local shopping center. Not only did we buy Alice's father the warm gloves she had requested for him, but also a scarf and a cap. I picked up several more surprises for the children. Then I asked Mother what she thought about buying a little tree. We prayed we weren't presuming too much, then went ahead and bought the tree, lights, and ornaments to decorate it.

Instead of resenting our second intrusion, the father cried when he saw the Christmas tree. "I wanted to get one," he said. "But with all the things we needed after the fire . . ." His voice trailed off.

That afternoon, Mother and I put aside our own holiday preparations as we helped the little girl and her dad decorate their tree. As we worked, we sang Christmas carols. After we finished the tree, Mother had a cup of tea and chatted with Alice's father while Alice and I slipped off to her bedroom to wrap her gifts and make a card for her dad.

When we left that day, I turned back to see Alice looking up at her dad and him smiling down at her. Then I looked at Mother, who was smiling and watching me. Suddenly I felt as if a huge weight had been lifted from my chest, and for the first time that Christmas season, I had a happy heart.

And I felt a soaring gladness
No language can impart,
For Love itself lay cradled
In the manger of my heart.
And a thousand bells were ringing
From a thousand towers tall
Glory to God in the highest!
And peace be unto all.

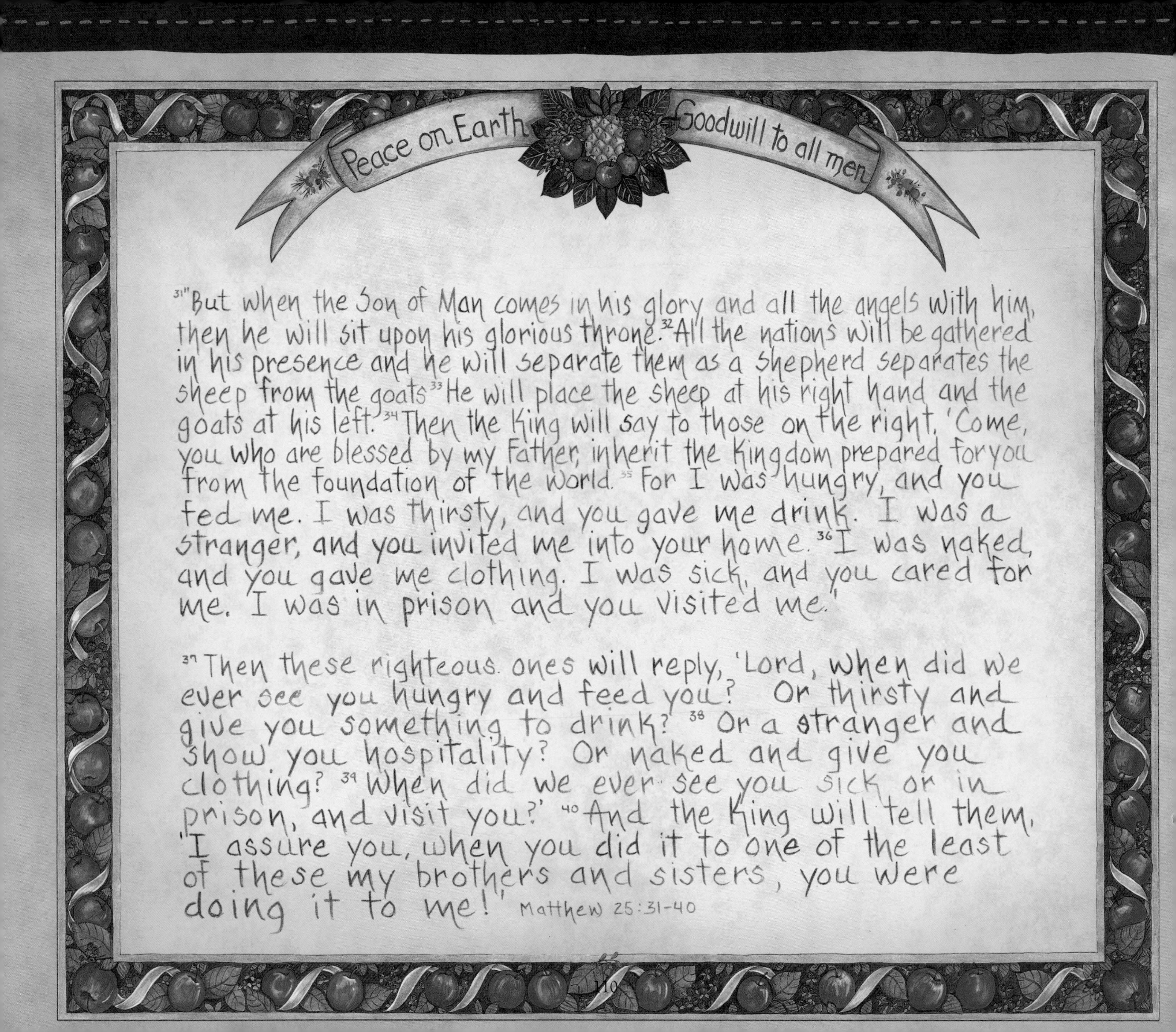

[31] "But when the Son of Man comes in his glory and all the angels with him, then he will sit upon his glorious throne. [32] All the nations will be gathered in his presence and he will separate them as a shepherd separates the sheep from the goats. [33] He will place the sheep at his right hand and the goats at his left. [34] Then the King will say to those on the right, 'Come, you who are blessed by my Father, inherit the Kingdom prepared for you from the foundation of the world. [35] For I was hungry, and you fed me. I was thirsty, and you gave me drink. I was a stranger, and you invited me into your home. [36] I was naked, and you gave me clothing. I was sick, and you cared for me. I was in prison and you visited me.'

[37] Then these righteous ones will reply, 'Lord, when did we ever see you hungry and feed you? Or thirsty and give you something to drink? [38] Or a stranger and show you hospitality? Or naked and give you clothing? [39] When did we ever see you sick or in prison, and visit you?' [40] And the King will tell them, 'I assure you, when you did it to one of the least of these my brothers and sisters, you were doing it to me!' Matthew 25:31-40

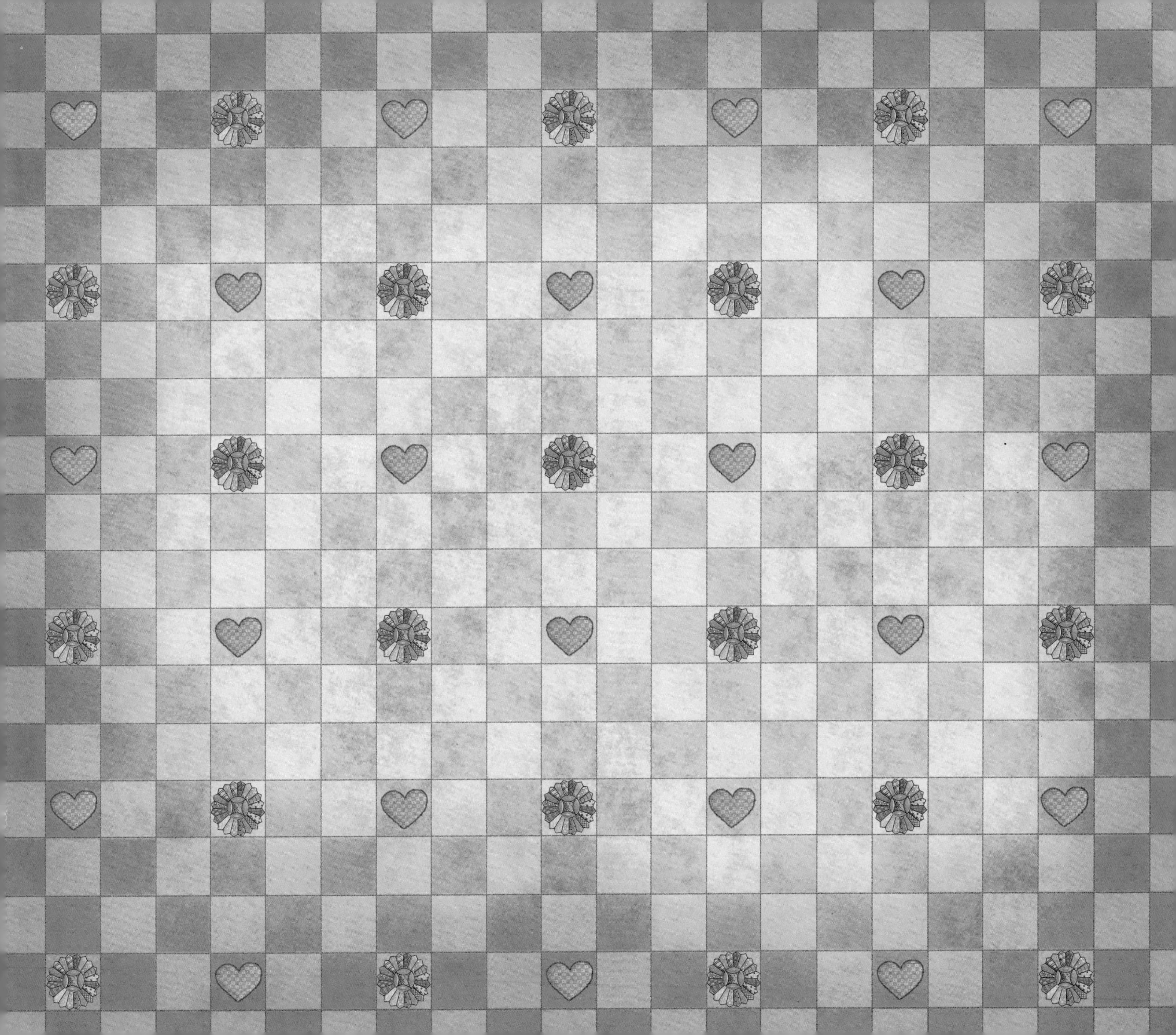

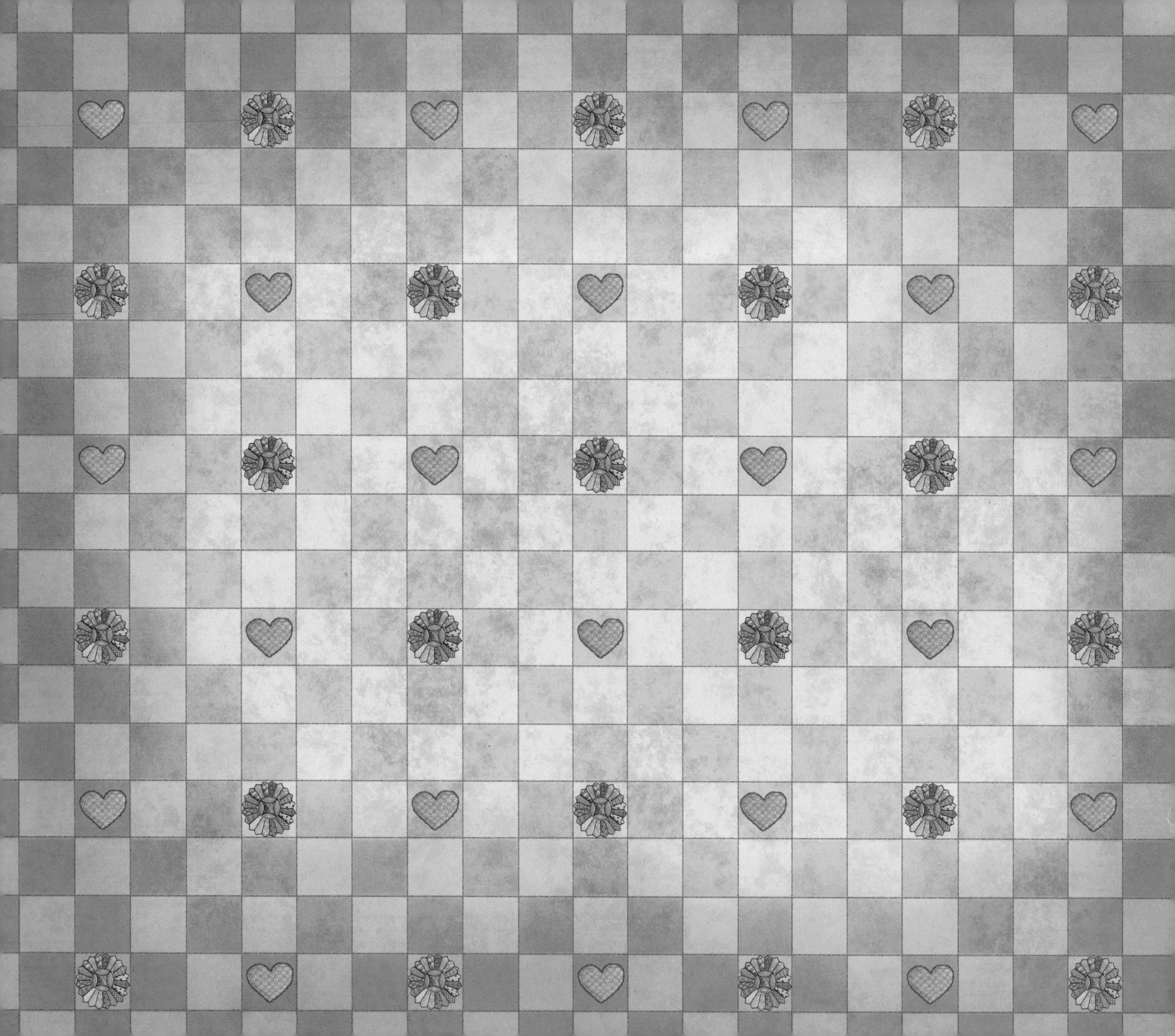